BEING &
Moral Persuasion:

A BOLT OF INSPIRATION

By

J.J. BHATT, Ph.D.

Two things move the mind with ever- increasing admiration and awe, the oftener and more steadily we reflect on them: the starry heavens above and the moral law within.

- Immanuel Kant

RECENT BOOKS* BY J.J. BHATT

HUMAN ENDEAVOR: *Essence & Mission/ A Call for Global Awakening.*

ROLLING SPIRITS: *Being Becoming /A Trilogy comprising nearly 550 poems.*

ODYSSEY OF THE DAMNED: *A Revolving Destiny.*

PARISHRAM: *Journey of the Human Spirits.*

TRIUMPH OF THE BOLD: *A Poetic Reality.*

THEATER OF WISDOM: *Essays on the Vedic Thought, Human Existence & Futuristic Prospects.*

MAGNIFICENT QUEST: *Life, Death & Eternity.*

ESSENCE OF INDIA: *A Comprehensive Perspective.*

ESSENCE OF CHINA: *Challenges & Possibilities.*

BEING & MORAL PERSUASION: *A Bolt of Inspiration.*

ONE, TWO, THREE...ETERNITY: *A Poetic Odyssey.*

REFLECTIONS, RECOLLECTIONS & EXPRESSIONS: *Selected Essays.*

* Available from Amazon and Kindle worldwide. Also visit: Amazon.com/author/jjbhatt

PREFACE

We human beings are endowed with an innate moral faculty that instinctly guides us to make choices between right and wrong. In this context, the great philosopher Socrates well understood human being must be the utmost consideration as he boldly declared, "Gnothi Seauton," meaning, "know thy self." For Socrates individual with right knowledge should make the right choices enabling to live a meaningful life with a reward of happiness. Indeed we know every moment of human existence is making of a choice and each having its own consequence.

Against this backdrop, *Being & Moral Persuasion: A Bolt of Inspiration* is presented as a fundamental message to the young generation that moral persuasion driven by rational choice is not a utopian notion but a concrete historical human experience and a viable strategy in-progress today. In fact, the act of moral persuasion is an eternal flame of human hope and inspiration leading toward an enlightened state of mind; facilitating our efforts to build a better world. In this respect, I have updated the book by inserting a new chapter 21 concerning the moral persuasion in action in 2017 and 2018.

Being & Moral Persuasion is also a timely reminder to the young people to assume their moral responsibility to save our global village and the magnifique planet. The well-known existentialist Soren Kierkegaard eloquently wrote, "There is nothing of which every man is as afraid as getting to know how much he is capable of doing and becoming."

J.J.Bhatt

Contents

1. INTRODUCTION

Only
In the beginning
Being shall ask
Where is his destiny?

Life must be a bolt of inspiration for every step of human endeavor that keeps going forward with time. During the course of this dynamic march, the fate of human existence greatly depends upon the choices we make and face the consequences there of. We have the power to shape life the way we want, if our personal and collective efforts are directed toward a good end. In that case, we are rewarded to live under a stable, order and peaceful conditions. If not, there is always the waiting world of suffering, pain and ignorance. It is in this context, the very act of executing our rational and moral effort defines, *Moral Persuasion* that is aimed at building a better world for us and for the coming generations to benefit in the future, whence the title of the book.

State of Modern Civilization

The historian Arnold Toynbee defined, "A civilization....as an endeavor to create a state of society in which the whole of mankind will be able to live together in harmony as a member of a single, all-inclusive family." In this respect, *Being & Moral Persuasion* reminds young people that great civilization is build by those who are optimistic and committed to their moral cause in fostering a better world. However it is equally important for them to know some of these glorious civilizations in the past were merely commas rather than long durable sentences of stability and peace. Toynbee also pointed out twenty-four civilizations did have their colossal rise and monumental fall during the long history of humankind.

The twenty-first century civilization is a vibrant, progressive and full of explosive advances virtually in all walks of life including the intellectual world of science, technology, medicine, arts and humanities to name a few.

Today we experience the collective consequences of modern progress in the form of globalization; defining our life styles and attitudes while we keep attending quotidian chores. However, on the flip side, there are number of challenges that have been brewing for some time and may prove to be fatal, if we continue to ignore them and fail to take necessary steps in time to alleviate them such as the climate change which governs existence of seven billion plus inhabitants and many other organisms on Earth.

Of course, there are other equally threatening on-going issues of our time we are collectively facing: nuclear proliferation, global terrorism and the rising tension among nations such as in the Korean peninsula, between NATO and Russian forces in Europe and the on-going violent conflicts in Syria, Iraq, and Yemen. Add to this list, frequent occurrence of droughts (an outcome of the climate change) in northern African nations: Somalia, Sudan, Chad and others forcing hundreds of thousands of 'climate refugees' to flee from ravages of hunger and death. Also, millions of displaced Syrians and

Iraqis caught in the war torn zones adding to the flow of migrations further compounding the situation in their neighboring countries of Jordan, Lebanon, and Turkey and lately in Europe.

Against this backdrop, it is important to take note of our contemporary civilization's asymmetric state as one third of humanity lives reasonably well while remaining more than two-thirds is struggling day to day to survive. This naked truth alone should open our eyes that global civilization is a sort of persona Dr. Jykel and Mr. Hyde. But the Janus reality cannot be sustained very long and it is time to change the course by way of bringing constructive measures that would prompt a collective and well coordinated action. Technology would be of great help, but ultimately it is humans who must make the right choices to rectify major issues as alluded.

The purpose of Being & *Moral Persuasion* is to let young people know that human beings are endowed with built-in moral and rational capacities giving them strength, hope and ability to meet their contemporary challenges head-on as mentioned.

It is also equally paramount that young generation must be made aware that behind their campaign of moral persuasion, there is a support team comprised of many dedicated scientists, technologists and non-governmental social guardians who also care for the welfare of humanity. Moreover, in view of the fact contemporary civilization is emblematic of the Age of Information, it is possible for young people to communicate with other youth on a worldwide level enabling them to set up a pragmatic strategy and in coordinating plans for how to resolve major societal and environmental issues of the twenty-first century. The poet Rumi has aptly expressed, "stop acting so small; you are the universe in ecstatic motion."

Age of Information

Since 1990s, there has been a phenomenal explosion in the unfolding story of humankind as it has undergone significant changes, for example from snail mails to the mercurial e-mails. The unprecedented techno-driven march aka 'Age of Information' has made it possible to connect humanity globally via social media, smart phones, AI-robots like IBM's "Watson" and so on leading to an imperceptible shrinking of the old wide world into an efficiently communicating petite Global Village.

It must be noted, rising population, people living longer and large scale human migrations due to drought, wars and poverty have increasingly crowded the modern Global Village. As a consequence, people of different ethnicity, diverse cultural and religious up-bringing and different point of views and attitudes are slowly assimilating in a relatively finite space of the Global Village, forcing us to adapt for the good of our survival as a species on this planet. The philosopher Henri Bergson aptly pointed out, "To exist is to change, to change is to mature, to mature is to go on creating one endlessly." It is time to change our collective attitude and fire up the spirit of moral persuasion to build a better world of tomorrow, *time is of the essence.*

Endeavor

We can't
Command
Neither time
Nor
Mortal event

Only moral
Endeavor
Shall make
Us free and
Nothing
Else will

That's the
Real worship,
Whatever
May be the
Brand of
Your belief...

Organization of the Book

Being & Moral Persuasion is organized into twenty chapters. Chapter 1 explores the general scope of moral persuasion within the framework of modern time. Chapters 2 through 6 probe the multiple aspects of the moral persuasion. Chapters 7 through 12 consider the fundamental message of each major religion emphasizing ethics and morality. Chapters 13 through 18 look into the dynamic act of moral persuasion beyond the realm of religiosity. Chapter 19 concerns with the issue of "relevance of being" and Chapter 20, highlights the general mission of moral persuasion benefiting humanity in the twenty-first century and beyond. The final chapter 21 updates the four episodes: *Women's March, Me Too movement, Carlottesville, VA* and the *March for our Lives*; illustrating moral persuasions in action in 2017 and 2018 in the still evolving United States of America.

2. MORAL PERSUASION

Only
In self-awareness,
We shall discover,
Our Truth.

Only the moral awakening driven by a rational understanding justifies why we exist? In fact, it is an opportunity to experience true freedom from ignorance, arrogance and indifferent attitude of corrupt and sinful human mind. It is in this ever unfolding drama of "good and evil," human beings have been struggling since the dawn of time. It is in this context, moral persuasion emerges as a potent force to ensure good triumphs over evil in the world. Moral persuasion is a human rational will to act either individually or collectively with the conviction to firmly stand against injustice that may exist in any form in order to protect the well being of humanity. It is a state of human determination and courage powered by moral and rational capacities to build a better world. In this respect, the act of moral persuasion is an absolute justification of why we exist as an intelligent being in this world? Moral persuasion is a measure of our collective integrity, hope and moral responsibility to define verily the meaning of who we are and what we may become.

The justification of the *Being & Moral Persuasion* also emerges from the fact that morality is a foundation of a good society. It is intricately interwoven with social conduct of people. John Dewey has aptly put it, "... moral judgment and moral responsibility are the work wrought in us by the social environment; signify that all morality is social...."

The social aspect of morality is demonstrated by the repeated collective moral persuasions of concerned citizens in the form of protest marches and rallies against prevalent injustice in the society, or against polluters who destroy quality of waters in a river or a lake. Morality in its dynamic form is moral persuasion which is expressed when a stern opposition by the public against corrupted politicians neglecting their duties for which they were elected, or to oppose an immoral war and so on.

Henry David Thoreau in his work, *Civil Disobedience* pointed out that the moral sense resides not in institutions but in individual person who acts on the basis of conscience. For Thoreau social change is brought about when the individual directly confronts the state and exercise his right. The protest rallies in the United States during the 1960s such as the Civil rights movement and a youth taking a bold stand against the war in Vietnam were powered by the spirit of moral persuasion intended to preserve the integrity of the nation's moral values and democratic ideals.

The action of moral persuasion never stops, it operates 24/7 and it is alive as people keep fighting for the improvement of human rights, women's dignity, income inequality, to eradicate exploitation of child labor and human trafficking and issues relating to environmental concern to name major ones.

Since its birth humanity has been constantly swirled around by the fire of moral persuasion every hour, every minute and every second and shall go on uninterruptedly for generations to come. Henry Miller said it well, "The world is not to be put in order incarnate. It is for us to harmonize with this order."

Shades of Moral Persuasion

Realistically speaking, the campaign of a moral persuasion has a relatively better chance to be effective in a state or a nation where people are educated, therefore well-informed and enjoy certain fundamental constitutional rights including civil and basic human rights allowing them to launch protest marches or rallies, if conducted in a non-violent manner, their voices would be heard and necessary measures would be undertaken to address the given situation under consideration. But a word of caution is in order since mass rallies also carry capricious burden of mob mentality, it has tendency to break-up into violence and in that case the authorities has the right to tighten-up their grip to quell the situation. In this respect, any campaign of moral persuasion requires discipline on the part of the participants to follow non-violent but well-disciplined conduct.

On the flip side, in a nation where basic civil and human rights are either ignored or non-existence, especially in an authoritarian regime, there protest marches or rallies face a stiff up-hill battle. As a typical illustration, the Tiananmen Square protest by the young people in Beijing, China in 1989 who were asking for democratic reforms were cruelly handled by the authority over there. In fact, the authority over there nervously overreacted to the event and hurriedly sent massive police force and several tanks killing hundreds of protesters. Also during the so-called "Arab Springs "in Egypt and anti-corruption protests in Brazil, Venezuela and Russia have suffered heavy handed treatment by the authorities.

The point being moral persuasion conducted either individually or collectively is neither perfect nor successful method in every situation.

That is why it is paramount to have a great deal of preparation on the part the participants in moral education and must be led by a competent leadership who possesses   an organizational skill to carry out an effective campaign. In the United States, during the 1960s, the hippies and the Black Panthers failed because there was no moral commitment in their respective movement. The former were victim to habits of drugs and promiscuity while the latter professed violent means to settle the score. Again, we witness today various groups of religious extremists that are engaged in terror-based violent campaigns lack the effective element of morality, consequently sealed the failure of their crusade. In the process at this writing, sadly some of these groups have succeeded in destroying their own precious heritage of once great civilization.

These few examples as alluded suffice to demonstrate the necessasity of having moral intention and rational understanding as the backbone while seeking a resolution to a given societal - based conflict. In absence of any

Attention

Time to
Wake up to
The Global call
Time to roll the
Moral ball

In unity
We shall
Endure
If not,
We shall
Perish in hell
For sure

Don't panic,
Just discover
Your
M*oral courage*
To meet the
Global call...

resolution to a given conflict, there would be always that senseless blood spilling and the endless cycle of violence, war and death by the big numbers. The action of moral persuasion may take a long time, but it would save lives of thousands upon thousands; avoiding mass-scale destruction of humanity.

Another challenge of moral persuasion is the thin line that emerge at times in distinguishing good from evil; giving rise to a moral ambiguity. The dropping of the atomic bombs in Nagasaki and Hiroshima is one such example where the issue was either to save more lives from a protracted war or kill relatively few by abruptly ending it. It is a subjective moral judgment and all depends upon how the issue of such a dilemma in question is articulated. If a leader is trustworthy and rational individual with compassion, there is a high possibility masses will support him by believing they were fighting for the greater good of humanity. However, any moral ambiguity is a nasty business as it never completely goes away either from the public opinion or from their memory.

3. Reflections on Morality

Without morality,
What is a being?

Indeed, morality and liberty do stand on the side of good, therefore an ever evolving expression of moral persuasion to take a firm stand against tyranny and injustice wherever and whenever they prevail, albeit it seems to be the leit *motif* of humankind's justification to exist. The Italian thinker Benedetto Croce rightfully wrote, "History is the story of morality and liberty." Keeping this important point in mind, let us briefly explore the illuminating theater of morality.

Morality deals with the principle of duty what we ought to do, thus making a choice between what is right or what is not in a given human situation. *Ethics* concerns with human conduct itself geared for a good life. *Moral persuasion* is defined as an instinctually prompted action by the individual's moral self that is his conscience.

Human integrity is an integral aspect of morality of an individual which is expressed through the fearless act of his or her moral persuasion. The human integrity has been illuminated by such historic figures: Buddha, Socrates and Lincoln and in the twentieth century, Gandhi, King, Jr. and many unsung heroes who worked so hard with great commitment to bring about positive changes to lift the dignity of their fellow beings. Ralph Wald Emerson wrote, "Nothing is at last sacred but the integrity of your own mind."

Moral responsibility is the foundation of moral persuasion as it emphasizes the basic duty of all able men and women to preserve good against evil in the world. The Good stands for moral and rational human potentialities possessing love, hope, goodwill, empathy and so on, whereas evil denotes human action motivated by envy, vanity, selfishness, greed, and his violent nature. Zarathustra, the founder of Zoroastrianism faith well understood the eternal conflict between *Ahura Mazda:* the Light meaning good and *Ahriman:* The Darkness implying evil. Similar warnings were echoed in the Bhagvad Gita and in the conceptualized vision of Armageddon. The modern world desperately needs to fight against evil which is manifest in rampant corruptions, greed and disrespecting the environment and other negative aspects that are collectively threatening the quality of life.

Evil in its strict sense is the consequence of humans' making wrong choices either personally or collectively that usually end up in mass suffering. Evil dwells in human mind only as mentioned in the form of envy, vanity, selfishness, greed all bundled up as ignorance, arrogance and indifference in attitude. Evil mindset, if not checked in time would lead to a greater possibility of hatred, violence, wars and even genocides. The human history is full of records of atrocities inflicted by mad imperial rulers, cunning priestly elites or ruthless dictators. In such evil driven world, the campaign of moral persuasion becomes an urgent challenge as it is the situation in modern time. Unfortunately, in view of the major challenges as pointed out in chapter 1, fate of modern world hangs under a Damocles' sword. It is time to take the moral responsibility to speed up the mission ensuring well-being of the seven billion plus citizens of the world.

Scientific Persuasion

Moral persuasion of the scientific community took a giant leap forward in the seventeenth century with creative and courageous works of Galileo, Copernicus, Kepler, Newton and others. These great minds took humanity beyond the rigid walls of the religious belief system and greatly helped in deepening understanding about the laws of nature. As we go forward in the nineteenth century, Charles Darwin, Russell Wallace, Gregory Mendel, Dmitri Mendeleev, Marie Curie and many great minds once again catapulted humanity farther into the ever expanding sphere of rational consciousness to grasp our biological and chemical roots and made us rationally aware of the physical world.

It was during the twentieth century, morally motivated and rationally driven thrust of human curiosity intensified when scientists, particularly Albert Einstein armed with his general theory of relativity educated the world about the notions of space-time, gravity, motion and so on; revolutionizing our overall understanding of the universe we live in. About the same time, scientists pursuing the field of quantum physics yielded new understanding about the subatomic realm and much later by inventors of the string theories began to expand human understanding regarding the nature and the general workings of the magnificent universe. At present, the scientific endeavor, albeit their collective moral persuasion is breath-takingly continues to probe deeper into the mysterious nature of subatomic particles, dark matter, dark energy, multi-universes and so on.

In this exponentially advancing "space age," humanity is already excitedly witnessing astounding beauty of the universe seen through the eyes of various space probes: *Hubblescope, Voyager, Kepler* and others. One of the noteworthy highlights of the space probes is the on-going odyssey of Voyager which has left the Solar system; enabling scientists to learn more about the mysteries of our galaxy Milky Way, the interstellar space and the enigmatic black holes.

Today, scientists are exploring the very fabric of matter and energy at its deepest level at Large Hadron Collider, (LHC), near Geneva in Switzerland. LHC is a complex architectural marvel as it has underground long tunnels some as long as 12 miles long. During the experiment, series of giant magnets accelerate the speed of two protons approaching from opposite directions (through the doughnut shape tunnel), allowing them to collide; generating enormous energies but only for a fraction of a second and recorded by detectors for further scientific studies. In recent times, using LHC experiment, scientists were able to discovered existence of so-called the "God Particle"aka the Higgs Particle; further deepening insight into our universe at a subatomic level.

One of the ambitious undertakings of scientific pursuits today is the U.S. plan to settle human colony on Mars sometime in the present century. Also the nation is in the process of sending a probe directly into the face of the Sun to closely study its Corona. The insatiable quest of the unknown conducted through the joint venture of the international community of scientists and engineers and others certainly is a mark of an excellent example of human moral persuasion in action in the twenty-first century.

Pursuit of Medial Sciences

The noble act of moral persuasion was highlighted when researchers completed the "Genome project" in the 1990s. It was, certainly one of the greatest milestones in the history of humankind. The continued studies of the Genome have helped in advancing the stem cell applications for a possible cure of various types of cancer and related diseases. Also medical research continues to look for possible cure for Alzheimer and other deadly diseases with a moral intention of helping patients to live a quality life.

Lately, an inspiring case of moral persuasion has been demonstrated in the well being of patients, for example veterans who suffered trauma in a war or others who were subjected to domestic cruelty. Now physicians can help such a person to recover by way of changing the neuronal pathways in the brain of the old bad memories; giving new life of happiness. Another shining historic example of the moral persuasion surfaced when Alexander Fleming discovered application of penicillin's to prevent polio and since then many other such prescriptive drugs have been discovered to ensure healthy life for humanity in general, and the quest goes on,

Recent advances in modern technology have been playing important role in improving the well being of patients who were paralyzed either in a war zone, auto accident or suffering from a stroke. Today employment of intelligent robots like IBM's "Watson "and others are assisting in keeping tab of millions of patient's medical records; processing the data with astonishingly high speed. Present day applications of AI-technology in the health related industry is in its embryonic stage and ways to go, but the bioengineers are pursuing research toward a healthy goal for humanity and that very endeavor is a quintessential act of moral persuasion.

Nature: A Best Healer

To be in harmony with nature is the best way to liberate oneself from the modern day stressful techno- addicted life. While living in complete tranquility of nature, a person can reinvigorate his or her moral energy. Indeed when the person breaths fresh air from the bucolic country living and spends a few moments of silence while walking through the grandeur of lush green forest, or enjoys smell of the fresh roses and experience calm in the spectacular beauty of motley colored garden, and listens to chirping of the birds in the early morning.... renews his spirit. To be periodically engrossed into the timelessness of nature means an opportunity to know our own being with clarity of thought;

leading to contemplation and in turn gaining deeper insight into what we call awakening of the moral self; the first spark of the moral persuasion indeed. Lao Tzu expressed it well, "When you know Nature as part of yourself, you will act in harmony. When you feel yourself part of Nature, you will live in harmony."

Morality of War

Morality of war on first impression represents sort of moral paradox, however on closer look; in certain situation it is justified. Dupre (2013) explained the concept of morality of war based on the principle of *jus ad bellum*, justice is to engage in war with good reason whereas the notion of *jus in bello* deals with the rules and conduct of the war defined by the International law: the Hague rules and Geneva conventions.

It is to be noted that from a historic point of view, some wars have been fought on the basis of *jus ad bellum* meaning, morally justified war as a just cause, for example the war between

Pandavas and Kauravas (as described in Bhagvad Gita), the constant conflict between Ahura Mazda and Ahriman emphasized by Zarthrusta and in modern time, the World War II. In each war, there was a narrative of friction between good and evil, and it was paramount to ensure the victory of good to permit continuity of humanity to live in a peaceful world.

Wherever in the world, there are humanitarians, seminarians and dedicated unsung heroes engaged in attempt to eradicate poverty, diseases, environmental degradation of air, water and soil and so on, offer us ever inspiring illustrations of the supreme moral capacity of human beings to change the world toward a good end. Emerson reminds us, "We want men and women who shall renovate life and our social state..."

Pages of...

On scanning
Pages from the
Long history and
Reading the
Great minds
I understood
There's so
Much to learn

Alas, there
Ain't much time
To fully grasp
Their depth,
Just a simple
Flashing thought:

What if humanity
Took their message
To the heart from
The very beginning?

4. Morality: A Historic Experience

I walk
Along the same trail,
Every day and I know
There is struggle & pain,
Still it's the right track
For my moral beginning.

Dawn of Morality

Interestingly, glowing spark of morality began ever since humans innately realized there was meaning to their existence in this world. This message was first dawn upon him when he first experienced the brilliant lightening and thunders in the mighty azure skies, saw the eye-blinding Sunrise and the golden Sunset, the awesome Moonlit and zillion stars ever illuminating the magnificent cosmos. These awesome displays of nature lead him to believe in a power that got to be much greater than him leading to the notion of God from these nature forces: the Sun God, the God of fire, God of sea, God of lightning and thunder and so on. Moreover to please these gods for a good harvest and protection against rival tribes, ancient beings began offering sacrifices of animal's even humans to please Him.

Interestingly, the oldest evidence of moral awareness comes from the anthropological sites with offerings of tools and meat (now left with bones) suggesting Neanderthals had spiritual propensity perhaps belief in afterlife. The Neanderthals lived between 250,000aqnd 35,000 years ago and for unknown reason vanished forever from the Earth. The Neanderthals lived in Europe, the Middle East and Asia. They lived either in caves or build hut-like structures and hunted big animals. Their brain size was 1300 cc remarkably comparable to modern humans.

Ancient Time

The modern humans *Homo sapiens*, is a relatively new comer on the scene as he emerged about 100,000 years ago. They have displayed moral instincts as seen in the paintings, for example in the ancient 20,000 years old cave of Lascaux, France.

Once the age of farming began about 10,000 years ago, human creative activities lead to birth of an organized religious belief, new customs, traditions and overall cultural identity. This new settled life style provided them with plentiful food and comfortable shelters; giving more time to contemplate, further sparking moral awakening. In particular, it was the rise of the priests class that managed affairs of the temple, in turn helping them to define the moral code of human conduct to sustain a cohesive farming community.

It is only through moral teachings in the name of god, priestly elites promoted stability, order and peace. Only in such a religious framework, peasants cooperated and put their collective labor for the agro-productivity of the community. When adequate supply of food, shelter and religious guidance were ensured,

FAMILY

We're
Not listening
To ourselves
We're
Not listening
To one another
We're
Family called
Humanity
But, we're
Not reasoning,
So well

Let's just
Learn to listen to
One another
Let morality of
Peace be in our
Rational thoughts
Let's just
Learn to save
The Global Village
We live in...

intelligent people of the community had time to invent ways and means of keeping tab of harvest by advancing knowledge of mathematics and learning how to grow best crops lead further progress in astronomy. All these timely innovative measures created conditions of prosperity and progress of the community. As the community grew and transformed into a city-state; planted seeds of an enlightened civilization. However, such well run civilized society fell prey to series of   attacks from the rival tribes that were not so productive leading to frequent warfares among them for the control of resources, notably food.

In time, when tribal communities became nations; the age old trait of war mongering continued in order to secure various resources: natural and human both. The sheer exploitation of Africa's natural resources: diamonds, gold and many others metals and non-metals by the colonial powers of the British, French, Dutch and others in the past are well known. One of the worse outcomes of the exploitation of the human resource was that of slavery of the Africans also well documented by the history.

An American and a onetime slave Frederick Douglass in the mid-nineteenth century undertook his campaign of moral persuasion to free his people from the jaws of slavery. One of the prevalent myths of the time, especially in the minds of the whites in the northern states was that while slaves were singing out in the cotton fields, the whites thought they looked happy. In order to erase the myth, Douglass wrote in his autobiography (1845) "The songs .... represent the sorrows of his heart.....as an aching heart relieved by its tears." The major objective of moral persuasion is to eliminate human ignorance layer by layer from local to global level.

5. Moral Awakening: Worldwide

Morality is the
True human potential.

The bolt of inspiration of moral persuasion struck the Hindu sages at the height of their contemplative state of minds when they heard the words of wisdom, *Shruti* over 5000 years ago in the Indus valley. The knowledge of Shruti subsequently led to the systematic development of moral education for generations to follow on the subcontinent of India; ensuring the integrity of its heritage, overall societal stability and a continued progress despite series of disrupting exogenous influences in much later part of the history. The solemn act of moral persuasion is best expressed in *Brihadaryanka* Upanishad: *Lead me from unreal to real, lead me from darkness to light, and lead me from death to immortality.* More on this topic is presented in chapter 7.

Another striking reality of moral persuasion shines in *Dhammapada* comprised of Buddha's teachings in the form of aphorisms and parables bringing forth moral pursuit of his own nature. Buddha so succinctly uttered, "All that we are is the result of what we have thought." "....hatred ceases by love." "Nirvana, the highest happiness...." He also emphasized, "...a well directed mind will do us greater service." For Buddha moral persuasion must be conducted through the practice of Noble Eightfold Path as treated in chapter 8.

The power of moral persuasion in Judaism is evident in the historic experience of Jewish people who came out of their captivity from Egypt lead by Prophet Moses. Moses was to take them to the "Promised land." However, to build an organized and a stable society in the Promise land, Moses intuitively underwent divine inspiration for having received the Ten Commandments which defined the basic code of ethics. He asked his people to strictly follow these Commandments in order to fine-tune their conduct thus to become cooperative and productive members of the Promised land. It was a moral necessity to secure a well coordinated manual labor for farming and related social and cultural activities to build a cohesive and a prosperous community, thus moral justification of the Ten Commandments.

In case of Christianity, moral persuasion is best demonstrated by Jesus Christ's Sermon on the Mount, his teaching of the Golden Rule and His personal sacrifice for the redemption of humanity's salvation. It is further presented in chapter 11.

Outside the realm of religious justifications of moral persuasion, we also read it vividly in the life and time of Socrates. Socrates lited the fire of moral persuasion as he asked Athenian youth to "know thyself." He insisted to cultivate virtues for ethical conduct which would lead to good knowledge; enabling them to make right choices, thus to attain self-fulfillment. The shining moment of his moral responsibility is illustrated in *Crito;* Plato describes how Socrates while serving his sentence was approached by

Crito and friends urging him to escape. At that point Socrates refused to do on the ground that being a responsible member of the society it was morally wrong for him to run away from the law. At that moment, Socrates advised them, "Think not of life and children first....but of justice first."

Plato in *Republic* presented Allegory of the Myth of the Cave to contrast two world of human existence: ignorance and that of enlightenment. In other words, human beings have freedom to make a choice either to live in the world of ignorance and be burden by a myopic outlook or be the participants of an open-minded and all-inclusive world of beauty, reason and morality?

Aristotle in *Nichomachean Ethics* wrote, "Every art and every inquiry, and similarly every action and pursuit, is thought to aim at some good, and for this reason the good....at which all things aim." Indeed, all human endeavors in life including moral and rational persuasion must be aimed at good, and that good is the ultimate justification of human existence for the sole purpose of building an enlightened society. Only in an enlightened society, there is durable stability, peace and harmony.

To attain good, Aristotle advised to cultivate virtues and for him "moderation" was among the best of all virtues. Interestingly, the Epicureans also held the pleasure principle to be moral and rational; permitting human beings to live a good life by freeing them from superstitions and fear of death.

Even the Stoic philosophers such as Epictetus (c.60CE) advocated the act of will can attain high degree of moral strength through self-control; enabling person to become an asset to the society. The Roman ruler and a stoic Marcus Aurelius (121-180) held the notion of moral unity in the world through the pathway of cultivation of virtues of wisdom, justice, fortitude and moderation.

Dialing forward, Immanuel Kant insisted morality is entirely within the individual, and that moral values upwelled from his will and purpose, whence the notion of *Intuitionism*. For him the realm of morality resides in the domain of rational good will and the will is individual's moral self acting in accordance with the operation of moral law. In this context, Kant put forward a criterion of morality called, *categorical imperative*, which states: "Act as if the principle from which you act were to become through your will a universal law of nature." Kant's morality is deontological meaning it must operate under all circumstances without exception. In contrast the British thinker Jeremy Bentham thought morality to be judged by the result of its action hence called the morality of consequence.

Friedrich Nietzsche (1844-1900) thought morality was depended upon human nature and to him which was not universally equal. So he introduced two sets of morality: *die heren* aka morality of the master or ruling class, and the *die herden*, morality of the slaves.

Nietzsche's die heren morality was based on the notion that existence is to fulfill human instincts, therefore the master morality is justified, especially for the ruling class. In contrast his morality of the slaves, the die herden was a direct criticism of the Judeo-Christian religion values that were committed to the protection of all members of the society including the weak and poor masses. Nietzsche argued that the Judeo-Christian teachings restrained impulsive and adventurous nature of the aristocrats to fulfill their potentials.

In his search for an ideal man, Nietzsche created notion of *Ubermensch* aka Superman. For Nietzsche his Superman renounced traditional morality of Judeo-Christian values and faith on one hand and as Stangroom and Garvey (2007) puts it, "....carving out his place according to his own will" on the other. The Nazis took Nietzsche's "Superman" notion to the heart and equated it with the madness of the superior race to be themselves and spread their propaganda to the German people during the 1930s and up to mid-1940s until defeated at the end of the World War II. However, that pseudo-myth of Ubermensch mania led by the Nazis

In Essence

Mind
Hanging
In between
Certainty and
Obscurity and
Not knowing
Right from wrong

Human
Endeavor
Is a must
To grasp the
Meaning
Within

Only for a
Brief moment
We shall see
Our
Moral image
In Truth
At
That point,
No question
Shall be
Left to ask...

Modified from *Magnificent Quest,*
Copyright ©2015 by J.J. Bhatt

resulted in 40 million deaths including 6 millions in the concentration camps. Humanity may well forgive, but never should forget such a heinous crime.

In the post-WW era, the existentialists in Europe offered sort of a new insight into morality relating to the notion of freedom implying human responsibility. One of the leading existentialists Jean Paul Sartre held, "existence precedes essence." Accordingly existence is true reality as individual make decisions while going through life experience. Making decisions gives him freedom, thus making choices means to define his reality. For this reason to Sartre human being is fully responsible for his action. That is why man in the state of existence defines his essence meaning, human nature.

6. Religion & Moral Persuasion

Let there be
Moment of silence,
Let there be
Flash of reckoning.

World religions constitute unique constellation of belief systems each looking through its own lenses toward a higher power, the Supreme Being or God. However, God has been geographically and historically known differently and worshipped differently in each orbit of a cultural tribal set up. It worked well when nations were far apart in their distances and predominantly comprised of virtually illiterate worshippers. Moreover, throughout history, in each tribe, an institutionalized religion emerged; allowing few priestly elites to wield their power and control over faithfuls; weakening the good intentions of the original messages of openness, inclusiveness and in sustaining a durable peace and harmony among all the people. If the guardians of the traditional religions were free of their religious provincialism, it is possible there would have prevailed a lasting stability, order and overall progress in the global society. Unfortunately, historical record speaks otherwise as the world periodically fell prey to number of religious warfares; often generating undesired consequences of chaos, rigidity and fanaticism leading to more violence, wars and death. Sadly, the trend continues today in the name of religion by a few zealots as if the old habit never dies.

We must understand human beings suffers out of fear and anxiety and need to take emotional refuge in the presence of an All Powerful, All Knowing Being to sooth such feelings of the unknown. In this respect religion play an important role in faithfull's life. However, the issue arises when institutionalized religions show tendency to infringe on the reasoning powers of others in order to sustain built-in biases, dogmas and holding the false sense of exclusive ownership of god and in imposing servitude, especially where faithfuls are virtually illiterate and poor. In that case all hell should break loose as a given religion defeats the very moral purpose upon which it stood.

In the present century, the traditional religion seems to be imperceptibly losing grip over numberof faithfuls, especially the educated men and women. As they live today in the age of multi-culturalism and globally-connected information, consequently possessing relatively better comparative understanding of the world's religious values. Naturally, these digitally savvy believers seek for right moral and rational fine tuning of their respective belief system which must be in accord with the new reality of the modern time. That is why it is pertinent to reexamine the essence of major traditional religions at deeper level of reality; eradicating superfluous flaws such as the tribal pseudo claim of monotheism, polytheism and atheism and an asinne claim of a geographic brand of god or gods.

Incidentally, polytheism holds belief in plurality of gods. Monotheism is based on oneness of God and atheism holds belief in non-existence of God. Let us see why these pseudo claims of monotheism, polytheism or atheism are irrelevant in modern age of reasoning. For example, the Hindus belief in God without attributes (Nirguna Brahman) is conceptually not different from those of Yahweh or God, the Father and the Holy Spirit. Moreover, religions that worship God with attributes include Jesus Christ (the Son of God) in Christianity and Hindus to the Saguna Brahman and the Trinity of Brahma-Shiva-Vishnu. At the same time, notion of atheism is the main theme of Buddhism. Buddha was not a God but a living human being who had grasped the "Perfect Wisdom." Confucianism affirmed, "Mandate of the Haven" without naming a specific God, and of course Taoism simply focused on living in harmony with nature.

Regardless of the existing differences of "isms," all religions share the same basic intention of how to transform an ignorant person into a good human being; ensuring stability, cohesiveness and overall peace in the community or the society. In order to achieve this noble goal, the belief of God is justified since faith gives hope and a necessary strength to endure through the vicissitudes of life. However, looking the concept of God from the optics of reasoning, we end up with a different kind of understanding as briefly described in the following section.

The Notion of God

We understand the topic of God's existence or no existence has been hotly debated throughout the history. There are traditional five ways of defending God's existence: (1) The etiological argument refers to the "First Cause "meaning everything that exist, or existed in the universe has a cause to initiate it; implying God' presence is necessary. (2) The ontological argument which is the instinctive thought or an idea of God itself, proving His presence in the world. (3) The cosmological argument rest on the observation of beauty and order in the universe proving there is an intelligent mind (God) who must have designed them. (4) The teleological argument holds that there is a purpose-driven intelligent principle ordering everything including inanimate things in the universe and such a being must be God, and (5) The axiological argument states very presence of moral values such as truth, beauty and goodness in the world proves God's existence

The acceptance or rejection of God is dependent either ones depth of belief or the power of reasoning. To a rational mind, God seems to be the mental conception of human being based on fear of the unknown which was derived from superstitions and ignorance. Perhaps God is simply a mythical object of the human mind. It must be noted number of thinkers like Schopenhauer, Nietzsche, Voltaire, Freud and others did not accept existence of God. Also atheists like Buddha, Mahavir and Confucius insisted let the human beings cultivate their moral attributes for the good of the society.

Our common sense dictates there can be only ONE Supreme Being, if one believes there is one in existence? But have we ever wondered God may be our cosmic optimism sustaining us in a constant state of curiosity of the unknown?

What if God is an intuitive assumption that instinctly sprung up in human whims in different locations at different times? And, what if God is simply nothing more than an ever enigmatic entity that sustains us in the hermetically sealed jar of puzzlement? What if God is an eternal teaser who dwells in our mind, but hides beyond our comprehension?

Rationally speaking, God may well be the psychological source of our guiding moral conviction and rational drive to grasp, "who we are and what we may become?" At deeper mental reality, what if God is our own essence? In the final analysis, if human being at the core is good, and whatever is good in human is verily a spark of moral awakening which is nothing but the actualization of moral self itself, a divinely attribute indeed! For this reason modern religion must focus on how to up well the flow of moral and rational potentials of its followers in order to help them evolve as enlightened human

HOLY MAN

While preaching,
Holy man
Kept rolling
Rosary through
His shaky fingers:

"Alas, there's
No peace,
The Divine is
Not coming"

A concerned man
Boldly declared:
Dear Holiness,
Journey is ours
To finish
Let our minds
Be disciplined;
Let our conduct
Shaped by
Good habits be
The power within

Only our sheer
Endeavor shall
Make us Divine;
Not these holy
Beads of rosary
Rolling through
These shaky teachings!

beings and encourage them to build an enlightened society where all people of the world would enjoy the godly peace and learn to live in harmony. British thinker John Stuart Mill appropriately thought of "religion of humanity" rather than one based on the worship of the Supernatural.

Finally, the old ways of branding of god or no god is not so relevant in the greater scheme of human experience, but what is so pragmatically important is that at deep level of reality, essence of all religions must be synergistic to strengthen human morality and encourage them to cultivate habits of ethics in order to foster a glorious global civilization in the twenty-first century. Bearing this in mind, let us consider basic positive aspects of world's religions in the following chapters 7 through 12.

7. The Vedic Point

*An awakened mind is
limitless possibilities.*

The Vedic point of view is founded on the
fundamental all-inclusive principle that moral
and rational potentiality of human beings is
universal and can be self-realized by any
member of humanity. The experience of self-
realization at deeper mental reality means every
person must diligently endeavor to evolve as an
enlightened spirit, thereby help in building a
better world. Keeping this basic point in mind
let us further probe into an ageless realm of the
Vedic wisdom.

Essence of Vedic Thought

One of the greatest gifts of moral persuasion
to the world is from the illuminating Vedic law of
Rit. The Rit boldly declares that the
moral law operates independent of any divine
agency in the universe. The moral law of Rit

The Vedic Spirit

When
The mind is
Awake & strong,
We can climb the
Mountain high
Anytime
We want

When
The spirit is
Strong,
We can reach
Distance stars
Anytime
We want

When
Belief in the
Self is moral
We can move
Mighty heavens
Anytime
We want...

grants complete freedom and full responsibility to human beings to rationally pursue efforts to make the world a better place to live in peace and harmony. This is the moral foundation of the Vedic truth which has endured over 5000 years, therefore carries a significant weight in the search of sustaining a cohesive and a peaceful global modern society.

Essence of Bhagvad Gita

As we explore the principle of Rit at deeper level, there emerge two action- oriented arms: *Dharma* (righteousness or duty) and *Karma* (law of action and consequence). The essences of dharma and karma have been incorporated in the *magnum opus, Bhagvad-Gita*. Dharma refers to the duty-oriented responsibility and karma is personal accountability of our thoughts, words and conduct. Basically, according to Bhagvad Gita, it is the performance of right duty and accountability that are at the core of sustaining an individual's character, family unity and overall social stability, harmony and peace.

The Bhagvad Gita conveys its message through the famous dialogue between Krishna and Arjuna that took place right on the battle field of Truth. The conversations between them is about moral self (Krishna) and empirical self (Arjuna). Krishna asked Arjuna to defend good by destroying evil that is present in whatever form including in human relationships: relatives, elders, mentors and others who stood on the dark side. Krishna is a metaphor of our moral self who insist to cleanse our Arjuna (that is, our empirically corrupted) minds that have fallen victim to apathy, fear, envy, vanity, selfishness, greed and ego; causing misery and suffering in the world. In this respect, Krishna's message to Arjuna: when good triumphs over evil, only then an enlightened civilization is a possibility. To realize this truth, it is incumbent upon all able citizens to fight for the Good of humankind. That is the fundamental social truth and moral responsibility of all human beings and that is the essence of Bhagvad Gita; indeed a pragmatic universal message to the modern world.

Rationale of Brahman

Brahman is an eternal existence and that which undergirds the reality. Although Brahman is one harmonious whole, have two manifests: *Saguna* one with attributes and *Naguna* one without. The Saguna Brahman is an empirical manifest of body, mind and spirit where as Naguna Brahman has no physical attributes, but an abstractive spirit that exist in human mind but not comprehended fully by him.

In regards to the concept of Brahman (also known,"Paratma"), let us consider the case in point of a moral persuasion lead by Sage Shankara (8th century). Shankara boldly declared *Atman is Paratma;* implying human being is a moral-self, aka "Atman" who is continually evolving toward an ever expanding moral consciousness, "Paratma." In essence, the statement, "Atman-Paratma" symbolizes a dynamic journey from a finite being (meaning atman with limited possibility) to become an enlightened moral being (meaning person of infinite possibilities); enabling him to work

Wisdom Eternal

Upanishad,
A fiery inspiration of
Every heart, mind and
Soul to be awakened
Brahman is the
Eternal existence;
There is no claim
To his name

Atman-Paratma:
Is the *leit motif*
A journey from
Ignorance to
Enlightenment
Moksa is the
Moral awakening,
That's Vedic wisdom
In a nutshell.

(Modified from *Rolling Spirits*,
Copyright © 2010 by J.J.Bhatt)

66

toward a good end, thus in building a better world of peace and harmony for humanity.

It was a rational flash of thought, *appercu* when Sage Shankara declared, *"Aham Brahman Asmi,"* that is "I am Brahman." He was attempting to explain that each human being must reach out to the unlimited moral and rational capabilities in becoming aware of the totality-of-all-experience. In essence, Shankara helped in boosting self-confidence of human beings and asked them to believe in their inherited moral and rational strengths to liberate themselves from the world of ignorance.

Shankara recognized the existence of moral-self, *atman* in every human being as his potential that must be actualized by becoming an enlightened being (*Paratma*)for the betterment of one's own self and in a larger perspective, for the sake of humanity itself. Shankara's doctrine based on the Vedantic wisdom was an inspiring journey from a finite human spirit (atman) to his full moral awakening comprised of infinite possibilities (Paratma); from ignorance to enlightenment, *sensu strictu.* This ageless message from Shankara seems to be valid today as it was during the c.8th century. In fact it is an ultimate quest, more appropriately a moral challenge to young men and women of the 21st century.

Power of Yoga & Meditation

Patanjali (Between 200BCE and 450CE) is the father of yoga and one of the pioneers of the technique of meditation. As a part of his moral persuasion, he proposed in his book *Yoga sutra,* how to build a healthy body and healthy mind through the consistent practice of yoga and meditation. He suggested when health is excellent so will the human spirit; allowing to absorb good thoughts, words of wisdom and to cater right conduct to live a meaningful and a healthy life. Patanjali's thesis make sense since it guide us how we should prepare ourselves to be healthy and well disciplined contributing members of the society. In this respect, the yoga doctrine is quite impressive as number of Vedic sages, Buddha, Mahavir, Ramakrishna, Vivakananda and Aurobindo to name a few who individually mastered the art of yoga and meditation; permitting them to undertake their respective moral persuasion to help sustain an overall spiritual heritage and a general societal stability on the Indian subcontinent.

Morality of Ramayana

Interestingly lesson from the epic of *Ramayana*, the story of Rama is noteworthy as it vividly demonstrated application of the moral law of Rit as mentioned. As a result, moral dilemma of life faced by the divine incarnate Rama in human form must be same as ordinary people suffering from grief and joy, love and hate, conflict of good and evil, *ad infinitum* aspects of existence itself.

In Ramayana, the drama unfolds when, Dasrath the king of Ayodhya (a city-state in northern India) while on a hunting chase was badly wounded and was on the verge of dying. However one of his queens named Kaikai saved him. The grateful king in return promised her a boon. After sometime, Kaikai approached the king and reminded him of his boon. The king Dasrath said, "Yes dear go ahead and tell me whatever you have in mind?" Then dear queen told him that he should make her son Bharat the heir to his kingdom and asked Rama, the eldest son to go live in exile for twelve long years. The king Dasrath was stupefied by what he heard, and fell unconscious and he never recovered.

When Rama learned of his father's dilemma, he assured the father that it was his dharma to abide by the queen Kaikai's demand. Rama without having a second thought instantly dropped his ambition of becoming a king and decided to live a life of a forest-dweller in a distant land. In the same vein, his lovely wife Sita insisted that it was her dharma to be with her husband, no matter whatever were the circumstances. Again she demonstrated her boundless love and moral commitment toward her life partner Rama without giving a second thought of sacrificing personal comforts of palatial life. Younger brother Laxman thought it was his dharma as well to stay with his big brother no matter whatever the consequences.

As the story evolves, while Rama, Sita and Laxman were in exile, Ravana, the evil king of Lanka kidnapped Sita through trickery. Rama had no choice but to take a bold stand and fight the immensely strong foe, Ravana in order to ensure the justice of good to prevail over evil. Rama had to kill evil incarnate Ravana and rescued Sita. It must be noted that during his exile, Rama along with Sita and Laxman had to undergo basic struggles of life. In particular as mentioned, Rama even though according to the belief was a God but had to obey the moral law of Rit like everyone else.

After completing their exile, Rama, Sita and Laxman returned to Ayodhya where Bharata (who never sat on the throne) was waiting for Rama to take over the rein of the kingdom. He too had to find a moral middleway to honor his mother Kaikai's wish on one hand, and to honor big brother Rama who he thought was the legitimate heir apparent to the throne of

Ayodhya. Indeed Bharata skillfully treaded his way through the narrow corridor of his dharma.

In Ramayana, Rama, Sita, Laxman and Bharata vividly illustrated selflessness, self-sacrifice and duty-oriented commitments that are vital ingredients of moral persuasion in maintaining a strong family unity and ensuring credibility and trust of the citizens of Ayodhya. Ramayana's message is clear: when families as the units of a given society practice moral values (dharma), it would sustain an enlightened societal experience to its participants as was the case in the Kingdom of Ayodhya.

8. Buddhist Point

Don't crave, don't tear,
Simply walk toward
Goodwill.

It took Gautama Buddha twelve long years to undergo the deep state of contemplation until he was hit by a bolt of inspiration to grasp why human suffering existed and how to rid of it. In turn that prompted Buddha, 'the awakened one' to identify four causes of suffering: (i) Suffering exist, (ii) There is a reason for it (iii) It can be rectified and (iv) There is a solution to it, "The Noble Eightfold Path."

Buddha's Noble Eightfold Path were cultivation of habit of good thoughts, words and deeds: (i) *right views*, (ii) *right intention*, (iii) *right speech* , (iv) *right action* (v) *right livelihood,* (vi) *right effort* (vii) *right mindfulness* and (viii) *right concentration.*

The mastering of the Noble Eight Paths is to strengthen three vital attributes: morality, wisdom and to focus on the path of moral persuasion leading to *nirvana*. Nirvana traditionally means extinguishing the negative desires and cravings, but should be understood as an act of helping others to reach a point of their individual moral awakening. Buddha sought nirvana for entire humanity to be liberated from the world of Dukha or suffering. In this respect, the notion of *Bodhisattva* is relevant.

Specifically, Bodhisattva refers to those awakened human minds who have postponed their entry into the state of nirvana until lifting all others to achieve the same; indeed this is a quintessential act of dharma driven by the spirit of moral persuasion. In modern time, nirvana and bodhisattva must be understood in cultivation of habits of good thought, word and deed to build a better world of peace and harmony among humankind, consequently to expand the sphere of goodwill, love, empathy, forgiveness and overall compassion.

In order to spread his message, Buddha established the egalitarian community called

Sangha. The Sangha admitted everyone irrespective of caste, class and gender. Basically the Sangha was based on core principle of 'inclusion. At the Sangha session, Buddha preached to his followers to respect women, to learn and listen to their elders, and children be guided well and be educated in virtues.

Interestingly, it is said Buddha was once asked by one of his followers at the Sangha session:
"What have you gained from meditation?"

Buddha replied, "Nothing!"He then proceeded, "...let me tell you what I have lost: anger, anxiety, sadness, insecurity and fear of old age."

The Sangha was one of the earliest multicultural and highly diversified groups of people who were drawn together to work toward a single purpose of achieving nirvana aka making of a better community and subsequently to expand it into an enlightened society. Sangha was Buddha's ethical experiment which sowed the seeds to build a moral society. The residual ingredients of such a peaceful moral societal behavior is witnessed in the Buddhist monk communities and their influence on the lay people in Tibet, in Dharamasala in India under the leadership of Dalai Lama, Laos, Cambodia and Thailand. In these nations, especially the monks and ordinary people conduct themselves with simplicity, humility and with great emphasis of living with an Ahimsa based life.

Moral Awakening: Emperor Asoka

Buddhist point of view especially its moral persuasion had a deep influence on one of the greatest Emperors of ancient India named, Asoka (209-232 BCE). Asoka launched a war against Kalinga (in modern state of Odessa) as an imperial strategy to expand his territory, The war was costly on both sides as Asoka witnessed thousands of human corpses littered all over the battlefield. He was shocked by the sight of 'mass killing field' and decided to refrain from such senseless violence and wars. He read Buddha's teaching of non-violence and decided to become a Buddhist.

NORTH COMPASS

Only from the
Power of
Character,
True
Rhythms of love,
Hope and laughter
Shall enriched his
Meaning

In the end,
Character is
Nirvana
Only then
Journey to
Truth shall
Begin...

Modified From *Triumph of the Bold,*
Copyright © 2014 by J.J. Bhatt

Asoka spread the message of Buddha throughout his empire and abroad to Sri Lanka, Thailand, Cambodia and various other places. It was the spark of moral lightening that fired up Asoka's very moral zeal that was so spontaneous and certainly helped changed the world of his time for good as evident from relative peace and overall stability that prevailed during his reign. Buddha and Asoka are quintessential examples which validate the veracity of the human spirit of moral persuasion as a powerful force positively impacting humanity.

9. Jainism & Sikhism

The power of
Compassion shall
Awaken all beings.

Vardhamana also known as Mahavir was a contemporary of Buddha. Vardhamana too traveled through the contemplative path and arrived at his own point of view; enriching Jainism as a moral religion.

The fundamental teaching of Jainism is avoidance of injury to any life; vigorously defending the principle of Ahimsa or non-violence. For Jains, the followers of Jainism, the goal of human existence is nothing but liberation from all bad karma referring to the evil human nature.

Jainism emphasizes the act of moral persuasion through the practice of five sacred vows: (i) *ahimsa (non-violence)*, (ii) *satya (truthfulness)*, (iii) *asteya (honesty)*, (iv) *sexual restraint* and (v) *non-possession*. The practioners of these vows would eventually free themselves from bad karma and at that point they would gain access to *Kevala*, an attainment of the perfect wisdom.

Final Quest

Let's just take
Baby steps to the
Temple of
Enlightenment
Yes, to the place of
Moral commitment

That is the realm of
Deep reality where
Ahimsa is the norm
That's where
Compassion is alive
That's where
Human is magnificent
And, larger than life
Yes, that's where
He is the divine
Himself...

(Modified from Magnificent *Quest*,
Copyright © 2015 by J.J. Bhatt)

In a nut shell Jainism focuses on the cultivation of good habits of thought, word

and deed in order to awaken one's own moral self.

For Jainism, it is the community of morally awakened spirits possessing wisdom or "Kevala" would have the necessary strength to build an enlightened society. This disciplinary approach to life by the followers of Jainism has resulted in their productive and morally-oriented contributions in the world of commerce and cultural enrichment in India and abroad. Mahatma Gandhi was greatly influenced by the principle of Ahimsa. In fact he eloquently expressed in his autobiography, "... the only means for the realization of Truth is Ahimsa." At the end of his autobiography he mentioned, "... in prayer to the God of Truth that He may grant me the boon of Ahimsa in mind, word and deed."

Sikhism's Point of View

Moral persuasion of Guru Nanak (1489-1539), the founder of Sikhism began with the affirmation in salvation through meditation of

Nam, the divine power. It is said God, the original Guru inspired his pupil Nanak with his sacred message and in turn he taught others about the divine spirit. The divine message was passed on until the death of tenth guru (teacher) and subsequently into the sacred scripture *Guru Granth Sahib* (Lord Teacher Book).

Sikhism's moral persuasion is reflected in its all inclusive belief which holds equality of humankind irrespective of caste, class or gender. Moreover it teaches that all humanity belongs to one race. The followers regularly read inspiring passages of wisdom from the sacred book of Granth Sahib, followed by *Kirtans* (prayers) and *langar*, a community lunch together with an attitude of gratitude to the Divine Lord and to strengthen bound of friendship and brotherhood among themselves and toward others.

The combined moral persuasion via respective teachings and practices of Vedic (Hinduism), Buddhism and Jainism and Sikhism have ensured an overall stability of a civil society in India throughout its history.

10. The Chinese Point

Mission of
Humanity must be
Harmony & Peace.

The Chinese point of view is primarily expressed through the writings of Confucius, Lao Tzu, Mencius, Mozi and Xunzi and others in regards how to fine tune human nature. In subsequent time when Buddhism was introduced by Zuxzang in China c. seventh century, Chinese culture was further enriched in spirituality. However, all of these schools were aimed at the welfare of the human beings by guiding how to live a balanced life: Confuscius emphasized harmony among people themselves in the society and Lao Tzu's Taoism focused on the spiritual harmony with nature. Buddhism complimented the other two as mentioned. Together Confucianism, Taoism and Buddhism defined the power of moral persuasion in the Chinese culture.

Confucius (551-479 BCE) mission was to transmit the social and political ideals that were prevalent during the early dynasty of the Zhou (also called Chou) rulers such as Wan, Ya and others who were examples of *te* or perfect rulers with wisdom and moral capacity. Confucius applied these benevolent rulers' ideals to the individual members of the Chinese society instructing them how to cultivate habits of moral and ethical conduct to build a stable and order society. Let us take a closer look at Confucius' model of how to upgrade human nature in the following pages.

Confucius teaching dealt with cultivation of *ren* (or jen) through the practice of *li* and *yi* defining the rules of conduct. Ren is the feeling of heartedness or kindness between individuals with respect and love. Specifically, ren is the basis of filial piety, wisdom, courage and loyalty to the ruler but more appropriately applied to the ordinary citizens of the society.

Li is the principle that regulated individual's relationship in family and society. Specifically li requires individuals to adhere to their proper social roles. Li helps in providing individuals to cultivate with social grace including paying respect to elders, senior colleagues and superiors occupying high positions. Also Li intends to cultivate good knowledge of religion and rituals. The concept of Yi defines the basic rules of conduct embracing right behavior at various levels: family, work place and in the society.

Together ren, li and yi define the moral character of an individual grooming him to become a virtuous person, *Chun Tzu*. To Confucius only people of Chun tzu attributes must occupy position of responsibility in the society. Incidentally, the notion of Chun tzu as previously mentioned is derived from the Zhou rulers Wan and Ya who had displayed excellent manners of virtue and benevolence in governing their subjects.

For Confucius if the society is ideally comprised of people possessing Chun tzu character there would be no need to govern the people, that is the society will run without imposing rules and regulations called, *wu wei*, meaning , no-action. Moreover, to Confucius, if the society is comprised of people of Chun tzu character there would emerge a *Great Sphere of Understanding* meaning there would be no conflicts; ensuring an overall societal harmony and peace.

In subsequent time, Confucius' scheme of moral persuasion to build a better society was further enriched by Mencius who emphasized the inherent 'goodness' of human nature. He essentially connected morality to human feelings as he taught about heart of compassion (ren); heart of shame (yi); heart of courtesy and modesty; heart of right and the spirit of wisdom.

In time, the momentum of moral persuasion continued as Mo tzu also known Mozi affirmed the principle of "universal love." Another thinker named Xunzi (also known Hsun tzu) advocated that human nature was evil that upwelled from uncontrolled desires and emotions. To improve the human nature he suggested "Artifice" in the form of passing effective laws, proper education and adhering to certain rituals. If these steps were successfully carried out, there was an opportunity for him to build a civil society.

Lao Tzu was an elderly contemporary of Confucius and who arrived at an opposite point of view regarding the state of human existence. Lao criticized Confucius' doctrine being 'artificial' since it lacked the notion of living an authentic life in harmony with nature as the best way to fulfill individual's life with a meaning. Lao tzu insisted in giving up Confucius' ren, li and yi all together to pursue life in a natural way of flowing with patterns of the universe. Lao Tzu's rejection of Confucianism is well expressed:

> *Pursuing learning every day*
> *more is acquired.*
> *Pursuing Tao every day*
> *more is dropped.*

Lao Tzu also best summed up the state of moral tranquility in these few words:

Be still and discover your peace.
Throughout nature everything in
the universe moves along, but each
returns to its source.
Returning to center is peace.
Find Tao by returning to source.

As mentioned in China, Buddhism was introduced by Xuanzang (600-664 CE) who had studied at the University of Nalanda in India. He spent twelve long years to study Buddhism and during this time he managed to translate 74 books into Chinese. He took the treasure trove of Buddhist wisdom to his homeland where it was welcomed by the rulers and people. Buddhism introduced utterly novel idea to the Chinese about the concept of hell, reincarnation and celibacy for monks. In time Buddhism was assimilated in the Chinese culture and in later was spread to Japan and Korea. In a broader perspective, the Chinese thought comprised mainly of Confucius doctrine along with Lao Tzu's Taoism and later by Buddhism are examples of moral persuasions to groom humans to live well in a stable society and in harmony with nature.

Triple Flavor

For Confucius,
Moral persuasion
Begins and ends
In person of
Chun Tzu with a
Power of *Ren*

Lao Tzu sought,
Tao, the Way of
Simplicity & peace
Add the spice of
Buddhist *Nirvana*,
Voila, we got the
Triple flavored
Inspirations to all...

11. Judeo-Christian Point

Through faith and
The bold journey of
Historic experience,
We have survived.

The Judeo-Christian religions are based on the premise of "God's will."These great religions emphasize human conduct in accordance with teachings of the Bible. The believers affirm that God's command must be obeyed since He is righteous and the sustainer of moral law. Christianity evolved from Judaism, hence appropriately we will first consider Judaism.

Smith (1991) mentioned, "According to the rabbinic view the Hebrew Bible contains no less 613 commandments that regulate human behavior." However the Jewish moral code is best known by the Ten Commandments which in fact constitute the moral foundation of Judaism and Christianity. The Ten Commandments emphasized: *Thou shalt not kill, thou shalt not steal, thou shalt not commit adultery, and thou shalt not bear false witness and* others.

The Aim

Let
These long
Struggles be the
Test of our
Faith

Let
Courage
Be the force of
Our survival

Let
Our people
Move on with
Inspiration to
Build a
Better world of
Peace and wonder.

The Jewish people were lead by Moses out of Egyptian captivity and had a big challenge of restarting new life in the Promise land. And for such a daunted task, it was paramount there was an input of moral persuasion by the people through observance of the Ten Commandments; enabling them to build a stable and order society in the Promised land.

Essence of Christianity

Moral persuasion in Christianity is chiefly driven by the awakened spirit of Jesus Christ. Jesus was a carpenter, teacher and a healer. He was born to resolve human suffering similar to what Buddha did for his people. Jesus' moral persuasion is best illustrated in His Sermon on the Mount: *Blessed are the meek for they shall inherit the earth....love your neighbors as yourself...whatsoever ye would that men should do unto you, do ye also unto them...Ye shall know the truth and truth shall make you free.*

To Jesus, happy people are meek, who weep, who are merciful and pure in heart. He asked followers to practice the Golden Rule, *Do unto others what you want them done unto you.* He asked them not to resist evil but to turn the other cheek. He even emphasized, love your enemies and bless those who curse you. His teaching makes sense when we realize Jesus' intention from a moral point of view that he wanted his people to free themselves from their

The Healer

Jesus is
The savior who
Awakened people
To love, to hope and
To have faith
He taught
Forgiveness, humility
And charity
He
Died to redeem
Humanity's sin
He
Illuminated
Wisdom of
Existence while
Living for a brief...

sinful minds filled with envy, vanity, quid pro quo attitude by cultivating habits of love, humility and charity. He rightly advised followers to build up morally strong mindsets to avoid the curse of "violence begets violence" and preached them to refrain from it.

In time, Jesus' teaching and healings earned him recognition as a prophet and news of his activities rapidly spread and that drew attention of the Roman authority and ultimately led to his crucifixion. His body was entombed, but on the third day he rose from the dead and appeared to his disciples and subsequently ascended to heaven to be with God the Father. It was Jesus' crucifixion and resurrection that led to the birth of Christianity. When Roman Emperor Constantine embraced it in the fourth century it became official state religion and soon after it spread throughout many parts of the world.

Christian rituals such as baptism, the Sabbath, the Eucharist, Mass, Easter and others facilitated indirectly moral persuasion of the followers. The papal power grew in time and contributed in maintaining over all stability of the Christendom for centuries, especially during the turbulent times when northern barbarians invaded richer parts of Europe. Moreover, the Christian guardians helped during the crusades and offered services at the time of epidemic of horrific disease of black plague in Europe. During the sixteenth century, Christianity underwent significant changes in view of the tumultuous age of reformation as it split into Roman Catholicism and Protestantism. Despite its share of highs and lows, Christianity as a religion has endured for past 2000 years and today it has the highest number of followers in the world. It is the Greek thought, Judeo-Christian belief and Roman canons define the foundation of the western civilization.

12. Islamic Point

Faith means
Mercy & Peace.

The religion of Islam means "surrender to the will of God." The Islamic teaching is centered on the Holy book of *Koran*. Its moral persuasion is founded on the adherence of the five practices by the faithfuls:

1. *Shadadah* or witness: to affirm, "I bear witness that there is no God but Allah."

2. *Salat* or prayer: the Koran requires prayers to be carried daily five times: at Sunrise, midday, afternoon, Sunset and evening. While praying followers must face toward Mecca and the Kabba which serve as the central focus point. Each day, muezzin (the prayer caller) invites the followers to pray these words:

God is great. I witness there is no god but God. I witness Mohammed is the prophet of God.

Rise to prayer. Rise to felicity. God is great.
There is no god but God.

These five times prayers are geared to keep faithfuls focused on life with a constant awareness of God's presence, thus avoiding misdeeds.

3. *Zakat* or alms:

Koran asks faithfuls to pay a required donation to charity. It lets the faithfuls not to forget the needy and the sick fellow beings.

4. *Swam* or fasting:

During the Month of Ramadan the faithfuls are required to fast, to refrain from smoking, drinking and bodily pleasures from dawn to dusk. Swam provide experience to the followers those who suffer from hunger and thirst. Also, fasting enable faithfuls to strengthen their will power. The end of the Ramadan is celebrated by the *Eid-al-Fitr* festival.
5. *Hajj* or pilgrimage:

Every Muslim is obliged once in a life time to go to the hajj permitting him to put aside worldly matters and commune with God. The destination of hajj is the Kabba centered in the courtyard of the Great Mosque in Mecca.

The religion of Islam intends to keep faithfuls on the right track through the practice of five duties: shahada, salah, zakat, swam and hajj to sustain moral persuasion for peace and harmony among people.

Prayer

In Essence
Faithfuls seek
Rahim (mercy) of
Him.
Through prayers,
Ramadan and hajj
They pursue
Peace & good will.

The Wonder of Sufism

One of the offshoots of Islam is the mystical path of "Sufism." The practioners of Sufism are called "Sufis" who are very much immersed in seeking inner purification. They preach love and compassion in pursuit of linking human beings with the Divine. Sufism emphasizes simplicity, prayers and fasting and their whirling dance called *dervishes* is a meditation in motion and an expression of worship called, *Sema.*

Jalal ad Rumi is a famous suffi who is well known for his beautiful poetry. In one of his poems, Rumi so aptly expressed, *there is morning inside you waiting to burst open into light.* In another poem he wrote: *Now is the time to unite the soul and the world. Now is the time to see the Sunlight dancing as one with the shadow.*

Another famous Sufi named Sant Kabir is well known on the Indian subcontinent for his devotional expressions called *bhajans* which are sang by people of different faiths to become better persons. Kabir's bhajans or prayers are popular as they are sang by millions of people: Hindus, Muslims, Sikhs and others with equal devotion and love. Kabir's poetry is timeless always kindling the moral instinct of human beings. In one of his poems Kabir expressed:

Slowly, slowly.... everything in own place happens. Gardner may water hundred buckets....fruits arrives only in season." In another poem he writes: *Listen my friend. He who loves understands.*

The great beauty of Sufism remains in its spirit of inclusiveness welcoming all people regardless of their gender, race, religious affiliation or whatever. Sufism simply urges people to come together as one humanity to pray, to dance, to meditate and to live peacefully as good human beings. In light of its simplicity and message of goodness, love and brotherhood, Sufism has excelled its devotional and love-based moral persuasion winning hearts of hundreds of millions of people on the subcontinent.

A Sphere of Understanding

Greene (2013) correctly pointed out, "What we lack....is a coherent global moral philosophy one that can resolve disagreements among competing moral tribes." For this reason it is germane to seek for a fundamental agreement among all religions to meet the symbiotic goal of building a peaceful and a stable world. Smith (1991) aptly put it, "We need the courage and profit from the wisdom traditions of mankind."

It is time to understand that all religions when collectively put to gather as a unified moral persuasion, it would manifest as one juggernaut force with a capability of bringing stability, peace and order in the world. It is time we acknowledge that each religion has given us among the great human beings: Christianity gave us Lincoln, King, Jr. and Mother Teresa; Islam gave Rumi and Sant Kabir; Hinduism gave the Vedic sages, Gandhi and Tagore and individually inspired: Buddha (Buddhism), Mahavir (Jainism), Guru Nanak (Sikhism); Confucius and Lao Tzu and million other dedicated unsung heroes who have made a significant difference for the betterment of humankind. In fact these great souls together have awakened and inspired subsequent generations to continue with the campaign of moral persuasion in order to lift human dignity and to sustain social stability and peace.

Against this backdrop, we must acknowledge the world religions are not separate, *substratum;* simply different point of views at the surface. It is time to integrate principal fundamental religious essences: *Rit, Dharma* and *Karma*; The *Noble Eight Paths*, *Ahimsa*, *The Ten Commandments*, *Sermon on Mount*, *Rahim*, *Ren* and *Tao* as our collective moral inspiration to secure a stable, well-order and peaceful world.

It is time we rationally understand world's religious teachings in terms of their collective power of transforming human potential into an actuality of a *Global Wisdom*. If this challenge is fulfilled, it would mark an apotheosis of human victory of moral maturity; giving true meaning to his existence, consequently leading to the reality of an enlightened society. In such an anticipated society, there would be no need of using the old destructive ways of "guns, bombs and missiles" to resolve the global challenges. In this respect, the significance of the world's religions is aptly spelled out by the American theologian Ninian Smart (1973) who has succinctly expressed:

The fact that human civilization is now so tightly knit that its every crisis sends ripples around the globe is one reason why the modern study of religion, with its emphasis on understanding rather than preaching is so important. Even if we do not agree with one another it is vital that we should at least understand one another. We have a long way to go in achieving this understanding, however, the importance of the modern study of religion has not on the whole, permeated fully to people's consciousness whether in academic life, government, the media or in business.

What is Religion?

If religion,
Transforms
Humans to be
Enlightened,
It's Essence
Must be morality;
We must accept it
Whole heartedly

If religion
Promotes well-being
Love and no malice,
It must be ethics;
We must welcome it

If religion
Permits to
Cleanse the mind
We must embrace
It, at once

If religion
Preaches
Hatred and violence
Let it burn by the
Moral awakening,
In an instant...

(Modified from *Magnificent Quest*,
Copyright © 2015 J.J. Bhatt)

13. Realm of Moral Persuasion

When
Darkness engulfs,
Why forget the
Inner light?

Moral persuasion means application of human rationality and ethical conduct for overall good of the society and to save the Planet Earth. Specifically, moral persuasion is an action prompted by the instinct of our moral-self to act for the benefit of humanity. Being and moral persuasion stands on the premise that each individual is a moral agent, therefore has a moral responsibility to ensure that good triumphs over evil in the world. To keep humanity out of the cesspool of violence, wars and genocides, in this context, moral persuasion seems to be the most effective way to sustain peace and harmony among people in the world.

Human Existence Today
The on-going phenomenon of globalization has greatly impacted human existence in modern

time. Essentially, globalization has proven to be Janus, to say the least as it has brought mixed results. On one hand, the material abundance has given birth to the "over consuming lifestyle" to the billion or two but leaving many billions behind in poverty. Moreover, the on-going techno-driven forces are imposing great deal of tension to the hundreds of millions to adapt to new technologies that is changing so frequently and the behemoth scaled exploitation of Earth's resources keep producing massive energy and material productions to support the world's increasingly 'shopaholic consumers' to meet their insatiable demands of million different products. The high degree of consumptions by the world society is severely damaging the planetary environment including triggering the climate change; an existential threat to most advanced organisms including our species that is the weakest among them to survive.

Today, the world desperately awaits morally spirited people of global citizenship to participate in worthy mission of building a world of simplicity. meaning to get away from the existing hedonistic and techno-addicted life style. It is time to embrace simplicity, soften-up selfishness and greed and start emphasizing humanity, instead. The process should begin at the family level; subsequently step by step let it evolve through the campaign of moral persuasion to the highest point of building an enlightened society.

The enlightened society in the present century must be comprised of morally motivated like-minded people to work, *esprit d'corp.* These young men and women would be the noble soldiers of sustaining stability, peace and harmony, especially of a challenging multi-cultural global village civilization. It must be equally pertinent that via the campaign of moral persuasion, such a global village society would be characterized by tolerance; understanding and acceptance of diversity as a norm and not an exception. In fact this is the core of the challenge to the young generations of the twenty-first century. It is great to note the spirit of moral persuasion has recently surfaced by the recent movement of the "Global Citizen" which stands for justice for all, eradication of extreme poverty by 2030, gender equality, women's empowerment and environmental concerns to name a few.

Being it is

We keep
Struggling
Through this
Patch of Life
We keep
Exploring
At all times

While
On the trail
We laugh,
We tear and
We stand-up
To defend the
Moral being,
That's what
Who we are...

14. Global Persuasions

Human existence is
But a blink of an eye
No time to wait...

The *leit motif* of moral persuasion is ubiquitous and can work wonders, especially when a benevolent ruler, a spiritual healer or a good leader holds the reign of power. For each one of them would motivate his or her people to guide them to the right path of rational and moral inspiring end. In this chapter, we will attempt to bring out few examples which would validate the noble mission of moral persuasion within the global perspective as follows:

Moral Persuasion: Human Instinct

During the Zhou dynasty in China, the great rulers such as Wan and Yan understood importance of building a good and stable society far away from violence, death and mass scale miseries suffered by the millions during the Warring States Period (Circa 480-222BCE). They realized one of the best ways to encourage their subjects was to educate them with the help of such outstanding teachers as Confucius, Lao Tzu, Mozi and others. The ruler also looked toward Han Fei's "legalism" as a means to efficiently govern. Their combined strategy seemed to have handsomely paid off as noted by the success of the so-called, "Hundred schools" which was basically a clustered of these great minds as mentioned and whose combined work permitted rise of elites who in turn helped in sustaining a viable and peaceful society while the Zhou dynasty ruled. In subsequent times, Confucianism had the greatest influence on the Chinese societal development as treated in chapter 9.

In India, it was the rein of Emperor Chandragupta along with his brilliant advisor Chanakya together planted seeds of rational and moral aspirations to build an efflorescent Hindu civilization. It was during Chandragupta's time considerable advances took place in astronomy, mathematics, philosophy, arts and crafts. In fact it brought a number of learned elites who in turn expanded the world of literature; making citizens aware of the value of moral and rational habits to sustain a great civil society. Emperor Chandragupta in his later years underwent a spiritual revolution himself as he walked off from the seductive imperial power and the luxurious palatial life; became an ordinary Jain monk. It is said, the emperor turned monk when he realized the value of non-violence, Ahimsa which is the fundamental bedrock of Jainism (see chapter 8).

Equally impressive is the story of Chandragupta's grandson Emperor Asoka who realized the meaninglessness of violence, mass scale miseries and deaths as a way of fighting wars. He too adopted the principle of Ahimsa, love, compassion preached by Buddhism. Asoka unlike his grandfather stayed as the ruler and through his imperial power was able to spread the message of Ahimsa and peace throughout his vast empire and also overseas.

Identity

Journey of
Beings is to
Wake-up and
Be the master of
Their destiny

Let
All beings be
Friends and
Not foes
Let
All beings be
Awakened
Souls and not
Fool's gold

Let the
Journey of
Precious beings
Be their
Noble Goal...

From *Magnificent Quest*,
Copyright©2015 by J.J. Bhatt

In Greece, it was King Pericles who encouraged great minds, especially ethically oriented and rationally powerful thinkers like Socrates, and later his pupil Plato and others. In time these great minds became the architects of Greek Thought. These great minds set the stage for major ideals of ethics, moral and rational reasoning. Moreover, the Greek thought eventually led to the emergence of democratic ideals in Europe and subsequently in the United Sates and in many other parts of the world. Democracy in its pure form is a noble consequence of the collective moral persuasion of people deciding to govern themselves. When good prevails over evil, democracy works well, if not, rampant corruption, greed and loss of civility would systematically erode its strength in time.

15. Historic Persuasions

Life is mercurial;
Still wondering,
When to wake up?

Abraham Lincoln's Courage

Moral persuasion is the determination of fearless men and women who stood tall and fought against the evil of injustice. For example, during the mid-19th century, it was Abraham Lincoln, the 16th president of the United States who confronted the twin crisis: to keep the nation united on one hand and to affirm the principle of human freedom by emancipating the slaves on the other. In order to accomplish his two-folded noble goal, Lincoln fought against number of odds including the bloody civil war, but he stood firm in his moral courage and was eventually triumphant in the end.

Abe Lincoln's moral persuasion was highlighted in his famous speech delivered in 1863 at the dedication of the Soldiers National Cemetery in Gettysburg, Pennsylvania as he expressed his morally motivated appeal to the defeated enemy and asked them to join in the overall meaningful goal of unification of the nation. Lincoln's historic; the Gettysburg Speech is as follows:

Four score and seven years ago our fathers brought forth on this continent a new nation, conceived in liberty, and dedicated to the proposition that all men are created equal.

Now we are engaged in a great civil war, testing that nation, or any nation so conceived and so dedicated, can long endure. We are not on a great battlefield of that war. We have come to dedicate a portion of that field, as a final resting place for those who here gave their lives that the nation might live. It is altogether fitting and proper that we should do this.

But in a larger sense, we cannot dedicate, we cannot consecrate, we cannot hallo this ground. The brave men, living and dead, who struggled here, have consecrated it, far above our poor power to add or detract. The world will little note, nor remember what we say here but it can never forget what they did here. It is for us living, rather to be dedicated here to the unfinished work which they have fought here have thus far so notably advanced. It is rather for us to be here dedicated to the great task remaining before us- that from these honored dead we take increased devotion to that cause for which they gave the last full measure of devotion- that we here highly resolve that these dead shall not have died in vain- that this nation, under God shall have a new birth of freedom-and that government of the people, by the people, for the people shall not perish from the earth.

It was during Lincoln's time, the onetime slave the African-American Frederic Douglas also fought against the issue of slavery on behalf of his people. He was a self-taught individual and had an extra-ordinary oratory skill that he used it well to communicate with the white Americans explaining the hellish plight of his people, especially those living in the south. Douglas' moral persuasion along with the support of Lincoln and number of awakened citizens resulted in the passage of civil right legislation of 1864. The successful outcome of Lincoln and Douglas' moral persuasions were the reality of the Reconstruction Amendments: XIII, XIV and XV.

The XIII Amendment stated that the United States Constitution abolished slavery and involuntary servitude, except as punishment for crime. The XIV Amendment emphasized that no state shall deprive any person of life, liberty, or property without due process of law; nor denies to any person within its jurisdiction the equal protection of the laws. The XV Amendment, section 1: The right of citizens of the United States to vote shall not be denied or abridged by the United States or by any state on account of race, color or previous condition of servitude.

Although the legislative victory was accomplished for the black Americans during the nineteenth century, took another hundred years to make further progress in the 1960s and onward. The struggle for racial equality still continues at this writing and seems ways to go.

Mahatma Gandhi's Satyagraha

In the 20th century, Mohandas K. Gandhi aka Mahatma Gandhi launched his fearless campaign of moral persuasion called, *Satyagraha*. The campaign of Satyagraha was driven by a firm but non-violent protest against the British raj in India during the "Quit India" movement between 1920s-1940s. Gandhi and his cohorts launched number of campaigns of moral persuasions aka Satyagraha which succeeded in mobilizing the Indian masses who unanimously demanded the British to end their rule in India for it was immoral, illegitimate and absolutely not desirable by the three hundred million people who sought their dignity and freedom. The British had no choice but to quit as they could not fight against the powerful force of moral persuasion backed by staggering over three hundred millions! Gandhi's moral persuasion inspired Rev. Martin Luther King, Jr to apply the method of non-violence and civil disobedience to his cause in the United States.

Rev. King, Jr's Challenge

Another great collective human success in moral persuasion came alive between 1950s and 1960s when the civil rights movement went into action in the United States. Noteworthy among its struggle for the racial equality began when young African American Rosa Parks, a seamstress who stood up on moral ground and refused to make her seat available to a white passenger on the bus. The city of Montgomery convicted Parks of violating the City ordinance. This bus incident was catapulted from a local to the national level when Reverend Martin Luther King, Jr got involved. Rev. King, Jr. launched a non-violent march to protest against such discriminatory policy of the city. He asked his people to boycott the bus rides. In 1956, the U.S. Supreme Court ruled segregation of the city was unconstitutional. Indeed that was one of the triumphs of moral persuasion sparked by the intrepid stand of Rosa Park, King Jr. and their supporters. Another milestone in the pursuit of justice on moral ground emerged on the American landscape when King, Jr continued with his non-violence tactics to challenge segregation in Birmingham, Alabama. The city authority arrested King, Jr. While serving his sentence, he wrote a letter in which he expressed his moral spirit, "Injustice anywhere is a threat to justice everywhere."

In 1963, King, Jr's famous speech, "I have a Dream" indeed reached out to the hearts and minds of millions not only in the United States but the world over. Dr. King, Jr speech was charged with emotions yet it was optimistic as he asked people to look into their soul and judge the validity of the moral issue before them:

I have the promised land. I may not get there with you. But I want you to know tonight that we as a people will go to the promise land. And I'm happy tonight; I do not fear any man. My eyes have seen the glory of the coming of the Lord.

Rev. King's moving speech was essentially a metaphor for truth and for that reason it was so effective in conveying his message to the world. In particular King, Jr's soul-searching speech fired-up the conscience of millions of good Americans to accept truth on moral and rational ground. Rev. King, Jr's concerted effort demonstrated practical power of moral persuasion aimed at sustaining the dignity of all human beings.

Under Rev.Martin Luther King, Jr's leadership number of civil rights legislations were passed in the U.S. Congress and subsequently signed by President Lyndon Johnson to become the Civil Rights law. These timely legislations opened the doors for black Americans for educational and therefore economic opportunities, thus resulted into the making of a new middle class since 1970s. However, the race relation remains one of the unresolved issues in the United States and the struggle for racial equality still continues as aptly expressed in the crying spirit of human beings, *we shall overcome someday....*

Moral Victory

When Lincoln was
Killed untimely
Grieved nation knew
What the man stood for and
World's never the same

When Susan B. Anthony
Stood up for women's right
Her soul was on fire
World's never the same

When Gandhi was
Kicked off from the train
His soul was on fire;
World's never the same

When King
Roared, "I've a dream"
His soul was on fire
World's never the same

When Mandela was
Locked up for long
His soul was on fire;
World's never the same...

Modified from *Rolling Spirits*,
Copyright ©2010 by J.J.Bhatt)

16. Moral Persuasion: Women

Woman is the light,
Love and hope.

The daring feminist movement in the United States is another striking example of moral persuasion in action. A century ago, Susan B. Anthony (1820-1906) fired the first shot from the silo demanding for women's rights to vote, known as *suffrage*. Susan Anthony and cohort Elizabeth Cady Stanton published newspaper "Revolution" to promote women's human right to vote and pressing to change the divorce laws that were unfavorable to women.

The newspaper, "Revolution" set the stage for the first women convention in 1848 in New York State. The convention produced eighteen propositions to alleviate unfair treatment of women including voting and a demand for equal opportunities for educational and employment.

Susan Anthony's fight did not stop just in the declaration of women's suffrage on a paper but took a bold step forward as she and other ladies went ahead and bravely voted for which they were arrested and fined the sum of $100. These calcitrant ladies refused to pay the penalty on the moral ground that they did not commit any crime instead simply exercised their rights guaranteed by the U.S. constitution to its citizens. They reasoned, "We the people...." to be understood being all the people (that is citizens) of the United States inclusive of both genders: men and women and not just the exclusive privileges given to white male citizens with property. Clearly their case stood well on the solid bed rock of moral and legal reasoning. The practical outcome of Susan B. Anthony and her supporters mission of moral persuasion was paid off as the Nineteenth Amendment to the United States Constitution was ratified in 1920 granting women the right to vote; marking a historic moral and legal victory.

Although it was a legislative victory, it was just a toe in the door. As a result, the suffrage campaign continued prompting another leap forward with establishment of the National Organization of Women (NOW) in the mid-1960s. New breed of women leaders emerged on the scene such as Betty Freidan, Gloria Steinem, Bella Abzug and others to continue their collective moral persuasion to secure women's right for equality.

One of the major goals of the 1960s and '70s campaign was to educate the general public, especially women through publication of books and articles addressing issues of women rights. Freidan's book, *The Feminine Mystique* (1963) challenged women to think they are worth more than just a wives and mothers. She asked them to regain their identity and to develop their potential to the fullest extent through exercising their rights.

Gloria Steinem, journalist and feminist activist once worked as an undercover Playboy bunny in a male dominant world where she first-hand experienced how women were looked upon by men as sort of walking sex objects and not appreciated as intelligent human beings. Steinem after witnessing such disrespectful behavior of men toward women... fired-up her moral spirit by launching publication of the magazine *Ms.* which drew public attention about the undesired treatment suffered by women in the male dominated world. She also expanded her moral persuasion by way of series of book publications: *Outrageous Acts and Everyday Rebellions* (1983), *Self Esteem: Revolution from within* (1992) and related articles. Steinem's work encouraged women not to suffer from low-esteem and pointed out it was not their fault but it was the system that was set-up against them by the male dominated society.

In the 1970s and there onward, NOW and other sister organizations continued their fight to gain the *Equal Rights Amendment (ERA)*. They are still fighting to secure equal pay for equal work, for women's equal civil rights and protection of abused women. Unfortunately, the women's struggle to secure ERA has not materialized so far in the United States.

At this writing, women's moral persuasion still continues for equality of salary paid to women doing equivalent or same type of professional work as men do. Women still suffers from sexual harassment in work places: corporate, military and academics. In the academics, female students are venerable in social settings at some Greek fraternity parties and in certain domestic situation as well.

At present, on-going moral persuasion of women is not just confined to the United States but it has become a worldwide struggle for women. Good news is that modern globally-linked internet would facilitate many millions of women to become aware of their human rights for education and job opportunity equal to the male gender. Unfortunately, still there are number of nations including Saudi Arabia where women rights are not fully recognized. It is a shame we live today in the techno-driven twenty-first century, and yet unable to fully accept the dignity of other half of humanity. After all we are talking about giving deserving respect to our

Moral Courage

When
Challenge's on
Women are
Ready to serve the
Nation with
Self-respect and pride
Indeed, they give up
Pleasures of
Family, love and life
To serve the nation with
Self-respect & pride

Women in uniform
Not afraid of rough
Terrain to fight

When sent
To the frontline,
They fight with
Courage & pride
Yes, women still
Fighting for their
Dignity & pride
Daily in life...

(Modified from *Rolling Spirits; Being Becoming*,
Copyright © 2010 J.J.Bhatt)

grandmothers, mothers, wives, sisters, daughters and grand-daughters. Women's struggle is also humanity's collective moral persuasion that is geared to turn this societal wrong into right in order to build an enlightened society.

According *The Guardian* (U.S. edition, January 2017) *Women's March* in Washington DC numbered whooping half a million to protest against then newly elected U.S. president Trump's inauguration. Also, there were two million protesters worldwide rallying for the dignity of women. Make no mistake about it the moral persuasion of women has become a worldwide growing phenomenon as their collective force is steadily securing well-deserved justice and dignity and demand for career equality. The women's moral persuasion is heading in the right direction as time and information technology is on their side. *Time* (January 29, 2018) reported whooping 4 million participated in the "Women's March." Further information about Womens's March is presented in chapter 21.

17. Global Challenges

Build not the wall,
Build bridges to secure
Better world of peace.

Before the 1990s, privileges of greater
mobility and many material comforts of life were
available only to a few select nations: the United
States, western Europe and Japan and few
others. Today globalization backed by rapidly
advancing technology along with the early 1990s
thaw between the United States and former
USSR opened up the world for commerce and
trade; ensuing an incredible phenomenon of
globalization. Globalization in turn, speeded up
economic rise of a few emerging nations like
China, India, Brazil and others; triggering rise of
the middle class, thus further accelerating
growth of the global economy.

Globalization although brought plethora of
material comforts to hundreds of millions across
the world, but miserably failed to awaken the
global consciousness. A global consciousness is to

seek a stable, safe and a peaceful world by sustaining a well balanced economic and environmental mode of lifestyle in modern time. To attain this lofty goal, we need good leaders and enlightened citizens who possess moral and rational spirits with a vision and determination to undertake necessary steps to resolve our societal and environmental issues and help manage humanity in its best possible way to live in this small Global Village in peace and harmony. The bottom line is no divine can save us from our troubles and miseries but our well-coordinated moral and rational human endeavors will. We must walk the path of good with an all-time awareness that moral responsibility is the foundation of our moral persuasion, thus to build an enlightened society.

Some Considerations

On a larger scale, globalization is a two-edged sword. It has been a blessing for tech-savvy people possessing an entrepreneurial and innovative spirits to become rich; concomitantly facilitating the corporation's handsome returns, which in turn rewarding the share holders and many investors. On the flip side, globalization is brutal to the middle class where millions of workers in labor-intensive manufacturing sectors such as autos, steel assembly plants and lately mining where they worked have become obsolete largely due to automation. Mr. Trump trying to revive the mining jobs but won't serve the purpose in a long-run in view of the growing employment opportunities in the sector of alternate forms of energy: solar and wind. It is happening already on a worldwide scale. Coal is one of the sources which emits green house gases; contributing to the climate change.

Word on Education

Ideally speaking, the purpose of education in the twenty-first century must be directed to bring forth the ethical human being, the person in whom moral and rational habits of mind are fully developed. In this context, a university must serve as an inspiring temple of universal knowledge and skills to ensure supply of intelligent and productive members to the society. It would be of a greatest value to the society, if moral education is incorporated in the academic curricula. Moral education would be formatted as a participatory activity in order to make it a practical experience for the students that would include serving as a volunteer in a food bank, assisting elderly, sick and poor either in the hospital or their residence, conducting inter-faith dialogues, help in launching campaign of moral persuasion involving local issues to name a few.

Moral Persuasion Today

During the 2016 U.S. national election, one of the presidential candidates Senator Bernie Sanders fearlessly spoke out about the existing grotesque and immoral income discrepancy between the rich and struggling working middle class and poor. Sanders along with Senator Elizabeth Warren and others still at this writing are demanding the U.S. Congress to address the issue of income inequality via appropriate tax reforms; enabling the middle class to regain its expected standard of living and also enable them to help their children's education at the university and college levels. For this very reason Mr. Sanders asked the government and academics to provide tuition-free college education to the young people.

It is the educational opportunity to the young people coming from middle class and those from poor families would help them to become the productive members of the society. A productive society has a better shot at achieving the inspiring goal of becoming an enlightened society.

Mr. Sanders and others also insisted that health insurance be made available to all citizens of the nation. For him health insurance and tuition-free educational opportunities to the young people were their human rights; that is where basic theme of moral persuasion becomes obvious. It makes moral and legal sense to honor educational and health rights of the citizens, hence the very success of democracy. If these noble goals as alluded are not attained, it would pave the path toward rise of oligarchy and plutocracy, weakening the spirit of democracy as Lincoln so firmly advocated: "of the people, by the people and for the people."

If the United States intends to remain as a super power in this century, it must engage with moral stand and rational approach in resolving major issues: income-inequality, lack of affordable education, lack of affordable health protection, increasingly deteriorating infrastructures, degrading environmental conditions, and the unsettled race relations including the immigration policy.

Moral Awakening Worldwide

It is true throughout life we are making choices individually or collectively with good intentions. The issue of morality ensues when individuals fail to keep the promise, for stealing, betrayal in a relationship or simply being obtuse to well-being of others and so on. In a larger perspective, the collective moral issues are relatively more complex, thus carry profound repercussions as vividly demonstrated by the two world wars (WW) of the twentieth century, where total of sixty million people died including six millions killed during the holocaust in WW II. At that point in history, the moral core of humanity awakened as the world community unanimously voiced its deep sentiment under a solemn commitment that was lucidly expressed in the United Nation's Charter (1945):

We the people of the United Nations determined to save succeeding generations from the scourge of war, which twice in our life time has brought untold sorrow to mankind and to affirm faith in fundamental human rights, in dignity and worth of the human person, in the equal right of men and women and of nations large and small.....to practice tolerance and are together in peace with one another as good neighbors, and to unite our strength to maintain international peace and security... have resolved to combine our efforts to accomplish these aims...

Unfortunately, since the post- WW II, number of big and small wars have burst opened like the blood spewing out of the arteries from various parts of the world : the Korean war, the

Vietnam war, periodic occurrence of genocides such as in Cambodia, Rwanda and the Balkans in recent times. Sadly at this writing, the blood keeps spilling in Afghanistan, Iraq, Syria, Yemen, Libya, Somalia and the tension keeps steadily building up in the Korean peninsula and the growing tension between NATO and Russian forces in Europe, and between the United States and China in regards the latter claiming the ownership of the man-made islands for military purpose in the South China sea. And, there are also on-going issues of radical terrorism, nuclear proliferation and increasing threat of the climate change forcing us to live in an insecured world.

After having gone through the long bloody history of humankind, it is time we as humanity must realize that hatred leads to violence and we get tangled into the meaningless cycles of violence; leading to more hatred and then more violence, *ad infinitum*. In other words, all our Global wisdom, our human endeavors and the very purpose of undertaking series of moral actions turn into urn from a hopelessly dead world of human existence. At that point we

CENTENNIAL

The unfinished
Business of WW1
Became WW2;
Once again
World was thrown
Into forty million
Deaths and mass
Destructions at
Its worst

Today, it's the
Weaponized world
So lethal can
Blow up humanity
In minutes
After
Hundred years of
WW One,
We still struggle
The same issue of
War & Peace!

become the members of the hell. A hellish dominion made exclusively by human action alone.

Given the contemporary scenario, it should become apparent there is a desperate need to look for an alternate way to resolve the rising global challenges. Among these challenges, the environmental concern stands out at the top.

18. Environment: A Moral Issue

Let me breathe this fresh air,
Let me drink this clean water,
Let me live in harmony with
Mother Earth.

Air we breathe, water we drink and the food we secure from the soil are life supporting ingredients, therefore paying attention to the general health of the planetary environment is a must. In fact, environment is verily an indispensable asset of sustaining humanity on this planet. In this respect, polluters of all kinds either big or small got no right whatsoever to violate this sacred law of human survival. Their negative actions must be considered public enemy number one and of course immoral. It must be the moral responsibility of all citizens of the world to take a firm stand to ensure we have basic rights to breathe clean air, to drink clean water and eat food from chemically-free soil. In this respect, there is a need to launch a global moral persuasion to protect our environment with sufficient traction especially against our heavily materially-oriented modern civilization.

Since 1970s the scientific world has been warning us about the gradually deteriorating conditions of the planetary environment. The American biologist Rachel Carson was among the earliest persons lucidly spelled out the issue of pollution in her classic book, *Silent Springs*. In time, other scientists also joined her in warning the systematic rise in the carbon dioxide emission from burning of fossil fuels causing "Green House Effect."

In the United States, in response to these environmental warnings along with the grave concern for nuclear testing's, constructions of many nuclear power plants and the not so full-proof storage of radioactive waste led to creation of the federal agency in the 1970s named, *Environmental Protection Agency* (EPA). About the same time, the *National Oceanic & Atmospheric Administration* (NOAA) was established to study the oceans and the atmosphere. Similar research institutions were also established in Britain, in Europe and later in number of other nations. The infrastructure of environmental institutions and their basic policies are now virtually established worldwide. At present, however the real challenge remains between the moral persuasion groups demanding for the protection of environment and those pushing for economic growth (even at the expense of environment).

The Climate Change

National Aeronautical and Space Administration (NASA) as of February of 2016 calculated average sea level rise of 3.41 mm per year. It is deceptively low number but when we consider that many low lying islands and coastal states have been already impacted. As the climate warms up because of increasing carbon emissions on a worldwide scale; thawing of Arctic and Antarctica will correspondingly increase, consequentially speeding up the sea level rise too. The writings are already on the wall as scientists have been overwhelmingly warning us it is not the question of if but when.

If the issue of climate change is not resolved in time, sea- level rise alone would force tens or even hundreds of millions of people to leave coastal - mega cities and flee toward the hinterlands. In the United States mass migration of people from low lying coastal states such as Louisiana, Mississippi, Florida and others to the hinterlands would be disastrous to think of. Moreover such nations like the Netherlands, Bangladesh and thousands of islands including Maldives, Marshall Islands and scores of others would drown under rising waters; forcing thousands or even many millions to flee to the mainland's. As a consequence, there would be intolerable living conditions in such a crowded world. In such a milieu people may resort to violence, mass looting and unbridle tribal warfares as a means of "survival of the fittest!" By then it may be a formidable task for the authorities to restore order, peace and stability in the small but dangerously crowded Global Village. What a bleak reality for our children to face, if humanity ends up in such a hellish place!

Unfortunately, environmental awakening seem to be overshadowed by the unstoppable march of globalization. Moreover nuclear emergence of Iran and North Korea, series of wars in the Middle East and fight against religious extremists to name a few are additional challenges yet to be fully tackled in the present century.

Given the aforementioned scenario, add to it the continued march of globalization which is systematically transforming the world into a large scale consumer-oriented civilization. As a result, massive exploitation of planetary natural resources: air, water, soil and so on along with accumulation of radioactive waste, increased water contamination, chemicals released by the manufacturers, the unbridle growth led by urbanization, automation and staggering usage of fossil-fuel based energy have collectively and cumulatively impacted the general quality of life.

Among these causes as mentioned, threat of the global climate change is the most urgent. The climate change is causing droughts in northern

Africa which in turn is forcing hundreds of thousands of *Climate refugees* to leave their homelands and end up in Europe; increasingly turning the continental Europe into an over-crowded place.

Moral Persuasion in Action

The scientific community has unanimously concluded the climate change is a fact and there is no debate left. The *Inter governmental Panel on Climate Change* (IPCC) comprised of 2000 scientists across the globe unanimously pointed out the danger from the rising carbon emission in the atmosphere. As an example, carbon dioxide amount in the atmosphere today has reached as high as 400 parts per million (ppm) from about 250 ppm in the 1950s.

In 2016, the world community held the so-called Paris Conference to take action to keep the world temperature 2 degrees Celsius (3.6 Fahrenheit degrees) below the pre-industrial level. Moreover, 2 degrees C is the maximum temperature rise the global ecosystem can absorb without causing serious damage. The global temperature rise above 2 degree C will increase rise in sea level as the glaciers and icebergs continue to thaw in the Arctic and Antarctica. Also, global warming will cause mass extinctions and increase both the frequency and intensification of hurricanes by the year 2100. The World Health Organization (WHO) estimates that there are 12.5 million deaths per annum worldwide due to the global warming. Number of experts warns us we are essentially running out of time.

In view of the growing danger of carbon emissions causing the climate change as alluded, an impressive 195 nations, virtually the whole world overwhelmingly responded to the Paris Climate Conference in 2016. The Paris accord called for necessary steps to curb the rising temperatures impacting the global climate. Unfortunately as of 2017, the United States opted out of this unprecedented moral persuasion on the part of the world community. Number of leading U.S. companies of global stature such as Apple, Microsoft, Face book, Google and others urged the present Trump administration to support the 192 nation's collective effort to protect the climate, but of no avail. The concerned citizens in the United States have raised opposition against the current U.S. administration's anti-environmental policy which has deregulated the coal burning, permitting oil-drillings including in the pristine area of Arctic and dismissing the climate change as a hoax.

In response to the U.S. decision not to support the Parish Climate accord triggered a massive protest, *People's Climate March* in several cities in April 29th 2017. The march in Washington DC was led by Al Gore, the former U.S.Vice-President and a leading environmentalist, billionaire Richard Bronson, Leonardo Da Caprio, a Hollywood actor and an environmentalist as well and several thousand unsung heroes. Together they demonstrated one more example of modern day moral persuasion in action intended for the good of the global society.

The objective of the said *Environmental March* aka moral persuasion is to preserve the global climate from further deterioration. The moral support to the Climate March is also evident in the collective voice of the Paris Climate accord where 192 nations stood hand-in-hand together except the United States, Syria and Nicaragua. In case of Nicaragua, it did not support for it thought the Paris accord was not tough enough. Recently three governors of California, New York and Washington State criticized the U.S. decision.

There is a general common sense based understanding that protection of global climate is a moral responsibility of all nations (which most nations have realized it, whence their collective support to the Paris Climate accord of 2016). A healthy global climate would greatly facilitate the business of millions of producers of the goods and services, and of course to the end beneficiaries, the global consumers. If the climate change is abated, it would help in reducing frequency of natural disasters and in turn permitting consumers to put more money in their pockets and ultimately benefiting growth of the world economy. In that strategic sense, the Paris Climate accord is a "win-win" situation to all parties concerned.

Suggested Measures

The best course to abate carbon emission is to scale down our dependency on the fossil-fuels and to expand the alternate forms of energy. In recent time, numberof leading nations have gradually transferring from fossil-fuel to the alternate forms of energy such as solar and wind to generate electricity. However, these sources still fall short of the dominant use of the fossil-fuels: coal, oil and gas. The combined solar and wind account for about 10% where as the fossil-fuel runs over 50 percentage! But, solar, wind and other sources of energy are steadily growing. Hopefully, by the middle of the century, autos, trains and someday even planes and ships would be exclusively run by the sole usage of electricity powered by solar and wind. Nonetheless, the present day attempt by concerned citizens in many parts of the world is to set up massive solar farms, wind farms and other alternate forms of energy; proving moral persuasion in action. But we have ways to go.

Moreover, other practical ways to save the planetary environment include planting millions of trees throughout the world. In this respect, late Ms.Wangari Mathis's moral persuasion in East Africa that called for "the Green Revolution "is notable (Bhatt 2011). Number of big corporations mainly run by the young leaders such as Google, Face Book, Amazon and others from Silicon valley's in California, New York ,Massachusetts and elsewhere in the United States have begun to use solar power and in some cases in setting up green gardens on the roof top of their buildings.

The power of moral persuasion can be greatly strengthened by the young people of today as exemplified by Miss Susan Wojcicki of YouTube who appeared on Public Television

THRUST FORWARD

Whatever
We conceive
Is not in the
Mind of God,
It's the mind of
Man, only

Let the brain
Take credit for
What we feel,
What
We conceive
And experience

It's time
To stop being
Big babies of
The Great Divine
Faith may be great
But, moral endeavor
Must remain supreme
In the end...

(PBS)'s Charlie Rose Show, May 15, 2017. In
that interview she expressed   the awesome
power of social media in educating people on a

global scale. Accordingly, her company is able to upload millions of contents and making them available via YouTube to the billion people. The company calls for a plan to double audience by opening a new market in India where 1.3 billion perspective consumers live. On a worldwide level, we are speaking of over seven billion people who would someday become aware of their environmental and moral responsibilities. Fortunately, the power of growing technologies: Artificial-Intelligence (AI), virtual reality (VR) and machine learning and then teaching other machines will give an added capability in the expansion of moral education as well. In this respect, the global communication networks would have a significant influence in strengthening the campaign of moral persuasion that may facilitate to clean up the planetary environment.

19. The Relevant Being

Let
Moral inspiration
Be my intention.

There is a potential energy of moral instinct stored in every individual who is motivated to be a better person; defining the very relevance of being in him or her, *sensu strictu.* It is the relevant being who accepts responsibility to undertake action-oriented moral persuasion to build a better world. The relevance of being is alive and well in his moral self, albeit he is the living force of reasoning dedicated to his noble mission of ensuring good to rein over evil in the world.

The relevant being is one who has prepared himself to take a stand against injustice everywhere. He is an effective agent of rational and moral voice and determined to

The Seed

What
We need today
To groom the
Young minds:

Critical thinking,
Encourage art of
Complex reasoning;
A solution-oriented
Mindset to tackle
The issues of today

Of course,
They must master
Basic career skills
But never fail to
Disciplined their
Moral being

In the end,
Great society is
Build by
Enlightened
Citizens only...

(From *Magnificent Quest*,
Copyright ©2015 J.J.Bhatt)

live above gluttonous hedonistic material life style and to be free from techno addiction.

Indeed, we human beings are social animals but it seems we are now become socio-techno animals! There is a need to bring balance of life in terms of social interactions among people; permitting to rejuvenate the forgotten humanity once we experienced before the dawn of techno-addiction age. It is time we begin a disciplined engagement with smart techno- skills for the material well-being of the society on one hand, and pursue a quality of life as human beings on the other. The relevant beings must strive for a balanced moral and material civilization in this century and beyond.

The Relevant Being

Being & Moral Persuasion intends to focus on the meaning of what is a human existence? What are the characteristics of an enlightened human spirit aka "Relevance of a being, today?" Bearing this in mind, let us explore certain aspects of what is the role of an awakened being aka *Relevant Being* in the modern world by considering the following eleven criteria:

1. *The Relevant Being is a scrupulous individual who understands his sole commitment in life is to be the driving force of the moral persuasion that would lead to building an enlightened society.*

2. *The Relevant Being is a caring and concerned citizen who puts concerted effort to promote understanding and tolerance among people, especially in a highly diversified humanity that is rapidly becoming new reality of the petite Global Village society of the 21st century.*

3. *The Relevant Being is aware that when institutionalized religions are emptied of their respective negative built-in dogmas, pseudo-claims of a given brand of god, notion of false superiority and tendency of exclusiveness, there shall emerge a supreme global moral force in brining humanity*

together for the noble goal of building a better world.

4. The Relevant Being is an environmentally conscious individual who would courageously demand for the prudent use of Earth's precious resources: air, water and soil and fearlessly take a firm stand to save the global climate.

5. The Relevant Being must acknowledge when moral responsibility is collectively assumed, it is the best way to sustain supremacy of Good over evil in the world at all time. In this respect, human personal faith, basic religious principles and beliefs well-justified, if these are applied from a rational point of view.

6. The Relevant Being is aware that evil dwells only in human mind: envy, vanity, greed, selfishness, lust, anger and so on all bundled up in the form of ignorance, arrogance and indifferent attitude; causing human pain and suffering in the world.

7. The Relevant Being is well disciplined individual focused in cultivation of good thoughts, words and in strengthening his courage, self-confidence, compassion, love, hope and the quick sense of forgiveness. He always extends respect to others.

8. The Relevant Being is aware at all time his moral strength and rational goodwill gives him meaning to his existence. When people ask him, "why should I be moral?"His responds, "if you're not you forsake your essential humanity."

9. The Relevant Being's noble mission in life is through the path of moral persuasion in order to eradicate fundamental societal and environmental ills: racial and gender-based discriminations, income inequality, environmental degradation, political corruptions, unjust wars and of course the senseless global terrorism to name a few.

10. The Relevant Being must be aware of the world history and he must demand the authorities to honor fundamental constitutional rights of the people, in responding to their concern over environmental, educational, health and other related issues that would help the middle class and poor people. He must insist in conveying a very important message to the guardians of the nation that the middle class is the backbone of democracy and the sustainer of economic well being of the society.

11. The Relevant Being must be engaged in encouraging people to be educated, well-informed and be the participatory citizens in order to build a collective voice for the campaign of moral persuasions aimed at the good of the society.

Self Evaluation Test

The following is a simple and volunteered test for those who may like to learn about their respective moral and rational potentiality. If interested, please respond to the following:

1. Write in 100 words how do you perceive yourself to be?

2. Write in 100 words what are your five strong attributes?

3. Write in 100 words what are your five weaknesses?

4. Write in 100 words what you want to be?

5. Write in 100 words what steps you will take to overcome your weaknesses as mentioned in # 3.

6. Write what steps will you take to be a better person? List five steps.

7. Write how do you conduct yourself with your parents, siblings, friends, mentors and/or supervisors?

8. Write the worst situation you experienced and how did you react to it at the time? How do you see it in retrospective today? (write 200 words)

9. Write how you conduct yourself in a relationship with other person you care for him or her. (200 words).

10. Write what is your worldview? How do you intend to participate in issue(s) that concern you the most? (200 words).

Upon completing all answers, the reader should put them aside for few days. He or she should read them again to give some serious thought. After a week or two, he should discuss the contents of answers with the family, trusted close friend or a teacher and try to learn their impression of him as a human being. How the world perceives him is a first step of self-realization. The second step is introspection and the third, to begin the process of cultivation or the self-preparation

Gift from Heaven

Just think
A seed turning
Into a bud;
A bud into
A bouquet of
Flowers
Expressing
Grandeur of
Its essence

When rugged
Mountain is
Chiseled by
Artist's passion
Voila,
There is an
Awesome image
Mesmerizing millions

When a child's
Groomed with
Morals and Ethics
He shall enhance
Humanity,
Par excellence...

(From *Magnificent Quest*,
Copyright ©2015 by J.J. Bhatt)

that involves in disciplining habit of thoughts, words and deeds. To attain this he should stick with daily activities: physical and spiritual (yoga, meditation, prayers), visualization and nature walk, and daily intake of right diet and always observe the affirmation, "I am born to be good." In time, he would realize, "who he is and what his moral and rational potentials are." This is one of the suggested ways for an individual to begin journey on a right path, but with one caveat, "moral persuasion is a long walk, indeed."

While going through the practice of cultivation of good thoughts, words and conduct as alluded, he must also give sufficient time to contemplation as he will gain deeper insight into various aspects of the Self : strength of his commitment to a choice of a given concern including education, environment and related societal issues.

The test is aimed in a way to make the individual to become aware he is a part of something greater than himself. That is the act of awakening of his long but meaningful journey in life. That is the critical decision for an individual in question to launch a long but meaningful journey in life.

20. Moral Persuasions: Synthesis

We're the
Creator of our
Collective destiny.

As already mentioned, our contemporary world has shrunk into a *petite Global Village* where interactions among people of all walks of life are increasingly becoming a new reality. Only moral and rational education would greatly help us to live in peace and harmony in this small village. It is paramount we change the course of our global strategy to ensure stability, peace and harmony among all the people of the world. And, of course clean air to breath, clean water to drink and a fertile soil to grow free of genetically-manipulated corps. It is time we begin to care for the future of our children and their children to live in a stable, environmentally safe and peaceful world.

Against this backdrop, let us keep in mind the basic 23 propositions intended for young readers to comprehend that human spirit is reflection of his morality and rationality, albeit the very meaning of existence itself.

Proposition 1

Let the young blood carry the torch of hope and courage as participatory citizens via their bold journey of moral persuasion to build an enlightened society. The enlightened society stands on the foundation of understanding, tolerance, inclusiveness, freedom, social justice and equality of its citizens. It is governed by morally-oriented and rationally- driven spirited men and women who care for global people including children to pursue a meaningful and peaceful life.

Proposition 2

In this modern *Global Village*, globalization although has delivered plethora of material comforts to hundreds of millions across the world, failed to awaken the global consciousness. Global consciousness is to seek a stable, safe and peaceful world. The collective campaign of moral persuasion should be focused on building such an enlightened society.

Proposition 3

Life must be pursued by a moral spirit and not with the habit of being a consummated materialistic person. It is never too late to begin with a moral and rational mindset of life in which we are the center of it all. A life must be aimed at benefiting others by sustaining human dignity, love and happiness. In this context, moral persuasion powered by rational drive is the vital force in realizing this noble goal.

Proposition 4

Morally perplexing situation arises where no guidance is present to direct human judgment either personally or collectively. For example, in the pre-Buddhist Chinese thought, there was no acknowledgment of "forgiveness," "purgatory or hell" or the practice of "celibacy" neither in Confucianism nor in Taoism. It was when

Buddhism was integrated; the Chinese point of view reached its moral and rational maturity. In the same vein, in the occidental culture, notably the Abrahamic faith, obedience to will of God, or the Command of God was more prominent as exemplified by Abraham's readiness to kill his son Isaac but did not consider the principle of Ahimsa or non-violence which is so fundamental to Buddhism and Jainism. Hinduism focused on the concept of soul whereas Buddhism rejected it. In spite of such genuine differences among various religions, there remains a common thread of moral persuasion, *substratum* as each has been focused on achieving an overall societal cohesiveness and sense of cultural identity and belongingness. This is the seed of hope which would permit awakened men and women to integrate good of all religions and turn them into one powerful moral force to chang the world for good.

Proposition 5

In reference to the proposition 4, it is time to free ourselves from the superfluous notions of monotheism versus polytheism and different brands of gods. It is a common sense, there got to be only One Supreme Being to meet the emotional need of the masses. God must be understood as a moral guiding principle and a rational power that directs human beings to preserve Good of humanity; not to get bogged down into the arguments about the conflicting "Godly provincialism."

Proposition 6

Being & Moral Persuasion points out only moral and rational understanding of human existence shall free humanity from its woes, ensuing from ignorance, arrogance and indifferent attitude of human themselves. What the world need is a rational integration of the Ten Commandments, the Vedic dharmic principles of duty, The Noble Eight Path of Buddha, Jain's Ahimsa, Confucian "Ren" and to live in harmony with nature of Tao and so forth to build a strong sense of *One Global Heritage,* albeit an inspiring depository of *Human Wisdom.* Since religion is a powerful emotive force, its original message of well being of humanity must be incorporated into any moral and rational framework aimed at good of the society.

Proposition 7

The meaning of world remains in the commitment of moral and rational men and women of the twenty-first century. In this respect, moral awareness based on reasoning is the survival kit of humanity; planting seeds of ethical conduct, constructive customs and conventions that would ensure societal stability. Plato well understood that good life is build on the foundation of harmony of the soul, thus tacitly implying the rational spirit of beings shall enable them to live well.

Proposition 8

Morality is a binding glue of a society; therefore it is paramount that moral education based on reasoning be a lifelong practicing experience. Specifically, in addition having a scientific knowledge and technological 'know-how,' there should be inclusion of moral science education as the third pillar. Only when this trio is coordinated, it is possible to supply highly techno-savvy and morally-oriented labor force that would greatly contribute toward making of an enlightened society.

Proposition 9

When we collectively grasp the power of our indispensible gift of moral-self, we shall gain a greater understanding of 'who we are and what we are capable of becoming?' At that point, we shall fully awaken to our moral consciousness and conduct ourselves to evolve toward a higher goal of life which is to build a better future for all.

Proposition 10

Ideally speaking, our collective hope and self-confidence must remain eternal and our human efforts aka moral persuasion must be effective everywhere in the world in order to curb evil. In absence of good, our world would be in the state of chaos, violence, wars and even genocides which would be not a safe place to let our children and theirs to live. It's time to wake up and act.

Proposition 11

Morally awakened and rationally driven young men and women have the best potential to get on the pathway to enlightenment because of their open-mindness, good health and high powered cognitive capacity. When they understand the depth and magnitude of existing challenges of societal issues: race relations, women's status in modern world, asinne religious frictions, environmental degradation including the climate change, income inequality and the plight of the middle class and so on, they would be prompted to undertake necessary steps to resolve them in order to build an enlightened society in the 21st century. The young mind must remember, only people of optimism and moral strength can build enlightened civilization.

Proposition 12

Morality is the ultimate reality and its foundation is reasoning, character and a positive attitude of a human being. In this respect, moral will is the essence of humans, therefore justifying their existence. Moral will is the moral force and an agent of change; a measure of their inner strength enabling to undertake moral persuasion for the good of the society.

Proposition 13

To create a lasting Great Sphere of Moral World must be the objective of humanity since only in such a place it is possible to sustain supremacy of good over evil, thus to live in such an illuminating and inspiring civilization. When all attributes of a human being are well integrated such as his morality, reasoning, creativity and commitment, it is possible for humanity to live in peace and harmony. Only then in such a grand sphere of morality, there shall rise the golden Sun of hope, love and good life. In absence of it, moral persuasion shall hit a steep climb, indeed.

Proposition 14

Human beings are essentially a walking Janus reality as they carry both killing instinct and the compassionate trait. That is why there is an eternal tough-of-war keeps going in his evolving brain. The struggle between good and evil inspires mythic imaginations, religious teachings and associated anecdotal communications. Zarathustra, the founder of Zoroastrianism dubbed these two nemeses: *Ahura Mazda* (the light meaning good) and *Ahriman* (the dark meaning evil). Also in modern time, George Lucas' series of "Star War" movies skillfully illustrated the eternal conflict between good and evil forces.

Proposition 15

Basically, it is the power of moral thought; rational goodwill and the right conduct that define person's character, albeit his "relevant being." Collectively speaking, it would help measure the quality of a given society by the percentage of the relevant beings living in it. Looking through the pages of history of the world, only a few relevant beings have illuminated civilizations. When these great souls inspired and mobilized the masses by the millions for good of the society, their particular civilization flourished. Whenever evil in the form of corrupt leaders, twisted religious propaganda, or a ruthless dictators took over, their respective society got heavy doses of violence, hatred and wars and ending in miseries, thus burial under the shifting sands of history.

Proposition 16

Our modern civilization is at a cross road either we collectively do something to make it right by applying moral and rational principles to build a better tomorrow, or we simply continue with the habits of excessive materiality and techno-addicted hedonistic life style while ignoring the imperceptible loss of civility, morality, rationality and the gradual degradation of the environment? In this context, it is imperative that through moral persuasion along with utilizing the modern technology, we make a concerted effort to walk on the right track to leave for future generations, a safe and healthy world

Proposition 17

The success of moral persuasion has been lucidly demonstrated by the historic works of such great sons and daughters of the world society: Socrates, Lincoln, Susan Anthony, Gandhi, King, Jr., Rosa Parks and millions unsung heroes. Their collective fearless stand on moral ground has inspired every generation of humankind and more important, reminding we have the same moral and rational capacities to become greater than ourselves. Ralph Waldo Emerson succinctly pointed out, "Nothing can bring you peace but the triumph of principles."

Proposition 18

The ultimate aim of moral persuasion is to overcome injustice which undermines human dignity and human rights. This has been the ageless issue of moral and rational concerns of human beings against the sinful men who have imposed evil conditions on humanity from time to time. This has been the dominant *leit motif* of the world history; continues today and will do in the future, whence the campaign of moral persuasion is a never ending mission of humanity.

Proposition 19

The material condition of humans has changed and not his fundamental nature, whence many of the global challenges have persisted. For this reason, it is paramount to awaken our respective moral-self by launching a bold campaign of moral persuasion to tackle various existing major societal and environmental challenges head-on. We have no choice but to take a firm moral stand on a rational ground since it is the existential threat in view of many challenges as mentioned in the aforementioned chapters.

Proposition 20

While on the march of the moral persuasion, participants must remain calm with an attitude of *sang froid*. In any crisis, maintaining confidence and trust of the supporters is vital to its success. Despite the stormy situation, the young participants must collectively stay focus with the set mission which is to seek the ultimate victory aimed at good of the society.

Proposition 21

It must be well understood by the young people that the campaign of moral persuasion is not a utopian notion, but a viable strategy; albeit the only gateway to restore the global collective sanity and to think about the future of their offspring's. The question is in what kind of world do they want to let them live either in a chaotic, violent and polluted one or the one where they will live in peace and harmony with others?

Proposition 22

We are essentially time travelers in this fascinating world of techno-driven civilization of the twenty-first century. Our collective journey is long ways to go, but we must begin it with rational and moral awakening now. Let us leave a memorable legacy for generations to come to enjoy this magnificent Planet Blue. Let us consecrate ourselves to be the first *moral global citizens* committed to build an enlightened society for our generations to come.

Proposition 23

On looking toward the future, presently humanity is on the cusp of planting seeds of our species on Mars, Moon or may be Europa in this century. In a distant future they may set up a few sophisticated colonies somewhere in the galaxy Milkyway may be? And who knows someday down the road hundreds of years from now would plant human colonies in various regions of the magnificent Universe? Hopefully, during their distant futuristic cosmic adventures, our descendants will keep alive the eternal spirit of moral persuasion to ensure ultimate meaning to their existence. If there is God, our future cosmic species at that moment shall stand on equal footings with Him, *veritatis splendor*.

HUMAN DIVINE!

He is enlightened
When On the path of
Reasoning,
And future
Belongs To him

Moral judgment;
Rational insight is
The pathway when
Man and Divine
Shall become
ONE...

21. Moral Persuasions Today

Often it is the fire of youth that sets the stage for moral action to bring about positive social and political change.

Emergence of few major moral crises in 2017 and 2018 in the United States warranted to update the contents of *Being & Moral Persuasions: A Bolt of Inspiration*, whence insertion of new chapter 21.

History has shown when the degree of injustice reaches a particular level of boiling point (that is intolerance), usually explodes with massive public outrage, especially by those who have been suffering for a long time. In this context, it is the four contemporary episodes vividly illustrates that moral persuasions are alive and in action today: the *Women's March*, *Me Too movement*, *the Charlottesville episode* and the latest *March for Our Lives* organized and led by the high school students from Parkland, Florida.

The Moral Episode 1

. Women's March 2017/2018

The Women's March was launched on January 21, 2017 to demand for women's rights, immigration reform, health reform, reproductive rights and the related issues. The protest was aimed at bringing a widespread awareness of the unresolved issues of the time. Moreover it was a massive protest against then newly elected U.S. President Trump because of according to Washington Post (January 21, 2017) "...Trump's divisive campaign and his disparagement of women, minorities and immigrants."

The Women's March in Washington D.C. turn out to be a worldwide rally in solidarity as several thousands of protesters gathered in major cities in support of it. The Post also reported that more than a million people participated in the globally driven rally, "...from London to Los Angeles, Paris to Park City, Utah, Miami to Melbourne, Australia."

The Women's March was renewed in January 21, 2018 in Las Vegas to keep the wheels into motion through the on-going campaign, *Power to the Polls* for the voter registration, especially to target swing states to register new voters and fight against the voter suppression laws that prevented many communities from voting. The purpose of the "Power to the Polls" is to bring about constructive and equitable social and political change beginning with the mid-term elections due in November 2018.

As a result of past two big time rallies, nearly 400 women have been planning to run for the House of Representatives and few for the Senate. Marie Solis (*Newsweek*, U.S. Edition, Sunday, March 25, 2018) headlined in her article: "Women's March of 2018 isn't about Trump it's about upending the entire political system."

Moral Episode 2:

The Charlottesville, VA Event

The Charlottesville episode began on August 11th and 12th 2017 when *The Unite the Right* rally to oppose the removal of a statue of Robert E. Lee, the confederate general of the Civil War during the 1860s from Emancipation Park in Charlottesville, Virginia. The Unite the Right group was lead by the far-right comprised of white Nationalists, White Supremacists, Neo-Confederates, Klansmen and Neo-Nazis. They marched with tiki-torches and chanted racists and anti-Semitic slogans and carried the Confederate flags.

The event turned violent when counter-protesters clashed with the Unite the Right group. One of the individuals connected with the right wing rammed his car into a crowd of counter-protesters killing a young lady and injuring several people. Unfortunately President Trump failed to criticize the right wing protesters, instead stated, "hatred, bigotry and violence on many sides." His comments implied moral equivalence between the White Supremacists and the counter-protesters. In other words, his stand on the issue was interpreted by the critics being sympathetic to the White Supremacists.

The Charlottesville incident is a part of a larger U.S. issue of seeking equality, liberty and dignity of all citizens in order to build a successful pluralistic society with democratic ideals in accordance with the U.S. Constitution. In order to achieve this noble goal, it is important that all symbols of slavery be eradicated in the nation including statues of those confederates who fought for its continuation during the Civil war. However, the descendents of the confederates oppose it on the ground these statues and confederate flag are expression of their heritage and history, thus be saved, whence the burst of the Charlottesville event. It is an emotive as well as moral issue on hand and it is going to be long way to go before any healing takes place. However, it is a good beginning to raise morally challenged issue as alluded in order to evolve the society toward an enlightened end, which is always good.

Moral Episode 3

March for Our Lives

On February 14, 2018, a mass shooting took place at Marjory Stoneman Douglas (MSD) High School in Parkland, Florida. Unfortunately seventeen innocent students and staffs were killed and many wounded. The crime was perpetrated by a 19 year old Nicolas Cruz. As a result of such a massive massacre, the MSD student took a firm stand to launch a campaign for gun reform in the United States. They organized by founding the advocacy group: *Never Again*. Their powerful campaign was boosted when Florida's governor signed a bill that raised the minimum age of buying rifles to 21, made provision for waiting periods and background checks. The bill also called for arming of qualified teachers and hiring school police and banned bump stocks. However, still much needed to be accomplished regarding the issue of gun reformed on a national level. To meet this challenge a rally *March for our Lives* "was held in Washington DC on March 24, 2018. It was organized and led by the MSD students and supported by many nationwide youth organizations .

The *March for our Lives* was quintessential demonstration of moral persuasion as hundreds of thousands of young people and supporters and as high as millions across the nation. There were also 800 rallies held in many cities in the world.

The march by the millions was against the gun violence that seemed to go beyond the orbit of the common sense. The young people between ages 9 and mostly 17 had enough of it. They unanimously challenged the U.S. politicians to act by reforming gun culture which would ensure safety of millions of school-goers. They unanimously insisted they want to go to school to learn and not to die by bunch of crazy shooters. One of the young men from MSD bravely spoke, "Welcome to the revolution." A nine year Yolanda Renee King, grand-daughter of the Civil Rights leader late-Reverend Martin

Luther King succinctly echoed: "I have a dream: enough is enough." But it was the young student from MSD; Emma Gonzalez captured the spirit of the whole rally when she stood silently streaming tears for several minutes signifying the time took to kill seventeen precious lives. She broke her silence by fearlessly declaring: "Fight for your lives before some else's job."

All young speakers expressed their genuine feelings as they spoke from the innermost part of their souls urging the authorities, notably the legislators to bring about necessary gun reforms which would ensure safety of all young people in the nation. The millennial generation seems to have awakened to the seriousness of the gun violence and its terrible consequences. Hope the legislators in Washington DC would positively respond by taking common sense driven constructive measures to protect the innocent lives of millions of young people who are the future of the nation.

These four contemporary U.S. based moral episodes as alluded are interconnected as they are unanimously demanding for a social and political change in the name of equality, safety and justice. Only when a nation makes a positive moral, social and political progress, it shall evolve toward an enlightened society wherein citizens shall enjoy living in a civilized society of stability, safety and harmony. I am of the belief that after all society is for safe guarding individual moral rights.

Let us never forget human life is greatly defined by our indomitable will, our rational judgment and moral strength. In the final analysis, moral persuasion if persistently applied in real life (as illustrated by number of examples including those of the contemporary protest rallies in this book) against the evil forces, the good shall triumph in the end. However, the collective human struggle shall be stubbornly challenging indeed *ad astra per aspera*, "to the stars through difficulties." But, taking the moral stand is worth fighting for it ensures human dignity, justice and freedom.

EPILOGUE

Being & Moral Persuasion is simply a message and not a doctrine. It is intended to awaken moral and rational spirits of the young people. It firmly affirms that every human being is an embodiment of moral-self, hence has the power to participate in the collective endeavor of moral persuasion to foster an enlightened society in the twenty-first century and beyond.

Being & Moral Persuasion is not meant to convey truth but to let the readers become aware that moral persuasion is not a utopian notion but on the contrary a vital survival kit of humanity and certainly major contributing force in making number of enlightened society after society from time to time in human history and it would do so today and will do in the future as well.

Being & Moral Persuasion affirms that moral-self is a shining light of all human beings, albeit defining their very essence. It advocates that all able bodied citizens take moral responsibility to ensure good prevails over evil in the world. Moreover in greater scheme of things of this fast moving, fast changing world, morality is the anchor of hope and a guarantor of better life for all and of course for the future generations to come.

Being & Moral Persuasion insist that moral self is the ultimate truth and must be validated once again by building an enlightened society in this century, especially for the sake of children and the subsequent generations to follow. T.S. Eliot eloquently expressed it, *and to make an end is to make a beginning.*

LEGACY

Let us
Collectively
Fulfill this
Noble
Experiment:

We're
Moral essence
Born in human
Experience

Let us
Hold hands
Let the
Journey begin
If not for us,
Let it be for
Our kids....

GLOSSARY

Bhagvad-Gita: The song of the Lord (Krishna). An important Hindu scripture; a part of the Great Epic, The Mahabharata.

Chun tzu: A person of highest virtue fit to hold a responsible position in the Chinese society.

Dharma: Relating to moral duty or righteousness.

Eucharist: To conduct the rite which Jesus initiated at the Last Supper, and later on became the central observation of the Christian church.

Hajj: Means pilgrimage. The pilgrimage to Mecca is last of the Five pillars of Islam and which every adult Muslim should perform at least once in life in his life.

Karma: The Law of cause and consequence relating to the human conduct in the world.

Kevala: Refers to the highest knowledge in Jainism.

Li: The Confucian principle which govern the conduct of individuals at the family and societal level. Li is a means to ren.

Nirvana:	Attending a highest psychological state of mind to overcome negative desires leading to liberation from misery and suffering.
Ren:	"Benevolence "or "human kindness." It is also called Jen.
Rit:	The Vedic view stating moral law which operates independent of any divine agency in the universe.
Salat:	(Arabic) means prayer. It is one of the Five pillars of Islam.
Sangha:	A Buddhist community. Also order of the monks.
Tao:	(Lao Tzu) means the way. A path to pursue life which is in harmony with nature.
Te:	(Chinese) "virtue, power or character."
Vedic:	(Sanskrit) meaning illuminated knowledge or wisdom.
Zakat:	The duty of alms-giving in Islam. One of the Five pillars of the religion.

REFERENCES

Bhatt, J.J., 2016, *Theater of Wisdom*, Amazon and Kindle.

Bhatt, J.J., 2011, *Human Endeavor: Essence & Mission/A Call for Global Awakening,* Amazon and Kindle.

Commins, S. & Linscott, R.N., *Man and Man: The Social Philosophers,* Random House, New York.

Conat, Sea, 2015, *The Gettysburg Address: Perspective in Lincoln's Greatest Speech*, Oxford University Press, New York.

Dupre, Ben, 2013, *50 Philosophy Ideas*, Barnes & Noble, New York.

Gandhi, M.K, 1993, Gandhi: *An Autobiography: The Story of My Experiment with Truth,* Beacon Press, Boston.

Glover, Jonathan, 2001, *Humanity: A Moral History of the Twentieth Century,* London.

Green, Ronald, M., 1988, *Religion & Moral Reason,* Oxford University Press, New York.

Greene, Joshua, 2013, *Moral Tribes*, The Pergmon Press, New York.

Kung Hans et al, 1986, *Christianity & World Religions*, Orbis Books, MaryKnoll, New York.

NASA, Web: oceanicservice.nasa.gov/facts/html,February 21, 2016.

Purtill, R.L.1976, *Thinking & Ethics*, Prentice-Hall, Englewood Cliffs, NJ.

Smart, Ninian, 1973, *Religious Experience of Mankind*, Fontana Library of Theology & Philosophy, New York.

Smith Houston, 1991, *The World's Religions*, Harper-San Francisco, CA.

Stangroom J. and Garvey J., 2007, *The Great Philosophers: From Socrates to Foucault*, Metro Books, and New York.

Index

JAGDISH J. BHATT brings forty-five years of academic experience and authorship of 60 publications including 20 books; encompassing the scientific and literary fields.

or more information visit:
Amazon.com/author/jjbhatt